ADVANCE PRAISE FOR *THE ART OF WRITING TECHNICAL BOOKS*

Peter Gregory has written a superb book on *The Art of Writing Technical Books*. This guide is a thorough but easily digestible read for the aspiring technical book author. Peter has written over 50 technical books and brings substantial credibility to this topic. Hence, **his ideas, suggestions, and workflow are on the mark** and will help a technical writer organize, write, and edit their book. Peter's approach to writing the next technical book is highly recommended! I wish I had his book before I wrote mine!

ERNIE HAYDEN

Career cybersecurity executive and author of *Critical Infrastructure Risk Assessment*

In this book, Peter does an amazing job covering many other aspects of writing, such as setting a writing schedule and legal issues like using material that may be copyrighted or understanding key points in negotiating a contract with a publisher. I find that even with all of my experience in writing books, I will still use Peter's *The Art of Writing Technical Books* as a guide and **highly recommend it to those of you who need a roadmap to get your mental idea out of your head and published.**

GARY HAYSLIP

Career cybersecurity executive and co-author of the *CISO Desk Reference Guide* series

Peter Gregory has produced something that authors have needed for years: a way to get started in the technical writing business as well as the concrete facts about how to make it successful. Peter covers not only the not-so-obvious things that every author should know about the technical writing process itself, but also some of the important things that nobody ever tells you about when you're getting into this business: the business side of it. From the writing process to legal and logistics info, to how you manage your books before, during and after they are published, Peter's book should be your *first* stop on the way to a successful technical writing career!

BOBBY ROGERS

Career cybersecurity executive and author of several books

Peter's experience writing books really shines through in this indispensable guide to writing technical books. It is the complete guide to consider everything you need to know related to the process of writing books professionally. Topics include everything from talking about publishers to self-publishing options. He includes pay expectations, schedules, your writing environment, ergonomics, and so forth. He provides practical advice on how to organize, write, provide graphics, and so on – even considering some legal traps that new authors should avoid. In short, **Peter has written an extremely useful, easy to read book that covers all aspects of the writing process.**

MATTHEW WEBSTER

Author of *Do No Harm: Protecting Connected Medical Devices, Healthcare, and Data From Hackers and Adversarial Nation States*

I wish I would have had Peter's book before I wrote my first one. **This is a great primer** from a prolific writer **for anyone interested in breaking into the field.**

DAWN DUNKERLEY

Author of several technical books

In his book, *The Art of Writing Technical Books*, **Peter covers all the bases of the writing and publishing workflow and maps them into a clear and logical process** that anyone sufficiently motivated can follow. He also shares many shortcuts and techniques from lessons he learned while writing and publishing 51 technical books. And he does all this in his classic easy-to-understand and approachable style.

MARC MENNINGER

Author of several books on cybersecurity

Peter Gregory is a leading technologist with a track record of publishing numerous bestsellers across several decades. He's put together all of his vast experience and best practices to provide **superb guidance for technology experts interested in sharing their expertise through authoring.**

WENDY RINALDI

Associate Publisher, McGraw Hill Professional | Technical

The Art of Writing Technical Books **covers all the steps, minefields, and joys of writing a technical book.** There are many types of books out there, but my experience is that there is a special satisfaction that comes from communicating technical concepts that expand the understanding of intelligent readers. This book is written in a way that is a force-multiplier and will advance a greater and deeper understanding of technical material. The outcome is that its presence will benefit a large number of individuals as well as society.

BILL HUGHES

Author of numerous technical books

A rich resource of inside knowledge for aspiring tech writers. In these pages, Peter Gregory gives access to his depth of understanding of the tech book writing world, only acquired by successful veteran expert writers in the industry. *The Art of Writing Technical Books* is a well-thought-out overview of all the essentials you need to know, from considerations before you begin to write, all the way to creating future editions. Highly recommend this essential book as the perfect jumpstart to writing tech-related books successfully.

CAROLE JELEN

VP/Literary Agent, Waterside Productions

Technical writing goes far beyond simple technical manuals and 'how-to' guides. It requires a rare combination of skill, creativity, self-discipline, and humility. Peter possesses all of these qualities and does a wonderful job imparting his knowledge and experience to his readers in this book.

LAWRENCE MILLER

Author of dozens of technical books

I've known Peter for a number of years, interacting with him on security panels, presentations and forums and I've been impressed with his breadth of knowledge and ability to communicate. **Working with Peter on a successful security book for Wiley Press was a great pleasure which I intend to repeat in the near future.** I encourage anyone reading this to contact me for a detailed recommendation.

MIKE SIMON

CTO, Critical Insight and author of several technical books

I enjoyed working with Peter on his book projects—**he's a fine and responsive writer.** I hope our paths will cross again someday.

DON MACLAREN

Owner, BOOKSCRAFT INC.

I have known Peter both personally and professionally over the past two decades, and know him to be very knowledgeable in many security- and technical-related topics. **Peter has a unique ability to take a topic and distill it into the most important aspects and communicate the topic in a manner which makes it obtainable and understandable** for all. I highly recommend his books and tech-related writing.

MICHAEL EISENBERG

Global CISO, Business Executive, USAF Veteran

Peter has written **a definitive and detailed guide for the aspiring author of technical books working with traditional publishers.** I wish it had been available back when I first considered becoming a published author. That said, I still picked up some great tips I plan to use when I write my next book.

KIP BOYLE

Author, *Fire Doesn't Innovate*

The Art of Writing Technical Books

The Art of Writing Technical Books

The Tools, Techniques, and Lifestyle of a Published Author

Peter H. Gregory
CISSP®, CISM®, CISA®, CRISC®, CDPSE®, CIPM®, DRCE, CCSK™

The Art of Writing Technical Books: The Tools, Techniques, and Lifestyle of a Published Author

Copyright © 2022 Peter H. Gregory. All rights reserved.

No part of this publication may be reproduced, stored, or transmitted in any form or by any means, including electronic, mechanical, photocopying, recording, scanning, or otherwise, without the written permission of the publisher. It is illegal to copy this book, post its contents on a website, or distribute its contents by any means without permission.

While every precaution has been taken in the preparation of this book, the author assumes no responsibility for errors or omissions, or for damages resulting from the use of the information contained herein.

All trademarks and copyrights mentioned herein are the possession of their respective owners, and Peter H. Gregory makes no claim of ownership by the mention of products that contain these marks.

ISBN-13: 978-1-957807-49-2 print edition
ISBN-13: 978-1-957807-50-8 ebook edition

Waterside Productions
2055 Oxford Ave
Cardiff, CA 92007
www.waterside.com

Tech Editor: Lisa Theobald
Copy Editor: Lisa Theobald
Proofreader: Madeleine Swart
Cover and Layout Artist: Peter H. Gregory
Indexer: Peter H. Gregory

Cover image © www.gograph.com / Saicle

Information has been obtained by Peter H. Gregory from sources believed to be reliable. However, because of the possibility of human or mechanical error by his sources, Peter H. Gregory does not guarantee the accuracy, adequacy, or completeness of any information and is not responsible for any errors or omissions of the results obtained from the use of such information.

To my beautiful children.

To aspiring authors who will someday influence many others.

CONTENTS AT A GLANCE

	ABOUT THE AUTHOR	xii
	ACKNOWLEDGMENTS	xiii
	PROLOGUE	xv
	INTRODUCTION	1
1	BEFORE YOU START	7
2	THE BOOK PROPOSAL	21
3	LEGAL AND LOGISTICS	39
4	THE WRITING PROCESS	65
5	THE REVISION PROCESS	107
6	AFTER PUBLICATION	123
7	WRITING SUBSEQUENT EDITIONS	131
	REFERENCES AND RESOURCES	141
	GLOSSARY	145
	INDEX	151

CONTENTS

ABOUT THE AUTHOR xii
ACKNOWLEDGMENTS xiii
PROLOGUE xv
INTRODUCTION 1
    Purpose of This Book 3
    How This Book Is Organized 4

1 BEFORE YOU START 7
    Don't Start Writing Yet 7
    Consider the Writing Lifestyle 9
    Know Why You Are Writing 11
    Define Your Book's Purpose 12
    Identify the Target Audience 13
    Define Your Book's Takeaways 14
    Create a Table of Contents 15
    Develop Your Writing Technique 16
    Consider a Literary Agent 19

2 THE BOOK PROPOSAL 21
    Title or Working Title 23
    Author Background 24
    Intended Audience 28
    Purpose 29
    Market and Competing Titles 30
    Shelf Life 31
    Table of Contents 32

    Illustrations 35
    Format 36
    Writing Schedule 36
    Advances and Royalties 37
    Confidentiality 37
    Circulating Your Proposal 38

3   LEGAL AND LOGISTICS *39*
    Publication Channels 39
    Negotiating Your Contract 41
    Information Sources 45
    Copyrights 47
    The Team 50
    Your Book and Your Day Job 60

4   THE WRITING PROCESS *65*
    Setting Up Your Tech 65
    Your Writing Schedule 73
    Getting Organized 74
    Formatting Document Files 76
    Keeping Track of Your Work 80
    Including Graphical Elements 86
    Updating Your TOC 93
    Co-authoring 94
    Content Protection 97

5   THE REVISION PROCESS *107*
    The Front Matter 107
    Keeping Track of Everything 109
    Working Through Revisions 113

6	AFTER PUBLICATION	123
	Celebrate!	123
	Unboxing Your Books	124
	Promoting Your Book	125
	Dealing with Errata	128
	Pirate Sites	130
7	WRITING SUBSEQUENT EDITIONS	131
	Contract Addendums	132
	Research for Subsequent Editions	132
	The Revision Process	134
	Language Translations	139

REFERENCES AND RESOURCES 141

GLOSSARY 145

INDEX 151

ABOUT THE AUTHOR

Peter H. Gregory, CIPM, CDPSE, CISM, CISA, CRISC, CISSP, DRCE, CCSK, is a 30-year career technologist and a cybersecurity and privacy leader in a telecommunications company. He has been developing and managing cybersecurity programs since 2002 and has been leading the development and testing of secure IT environments since 1990. Peter has also spent many years as a software engineer and architect, systems engineer, network engineer, and security engineer. He has written many books, articles, whitepapers, user manuals, processes, and procedures throughout his career, and he has conducted numerous lectures, training classes, seminars, and university courses.

Peter is the author of more than 50 books about information security and technology, including *Solaris Security*, *CISM Certified Information Security Manager All-in-One Exam Guide*, *CISA Certified Information Systems Auditor All-in-One Exam Guide*, and *Chromebook For Dummies*. He has spoken at numerous industry conferences, including RSA, Interop, (ISC)² Congress, ISACA CACS, SecureWorld Expo, West Coast Security Forum, IP3, Tech Junction, Source, Society for Information Management, the Washington Technology Industry Association, and InfraGard.

Peter serves on advisory boards for cybersecurity education programs at the University of Washington and University of South Florida. He was the lead instructor for nine years in the University of Washington certificate program in applied cybersecurity, a former board member of the Washington State chapter of InfraGard, and a founding member of the Pacific CISO Forum. A 2008 graduate of the FBI National Citizens' Academy, he is a member of the FBI National Citizens' Academy Alumni Association, ISACA, (ISC)², IAPP, CyberEdBoard, and the Forbes Technology Council.

Peter resides with his family in Washington State and can be found online at www.peterhgregory.com.

ACKNOWLEDGMENTS

Writing this book began as a formal project in April 2021, but was in the making long before that. From April 2021 until now, writing and perfecting *The Art of Writing Technical Books* has been a team project with several who helped along the way.

Appreciation to several long-time associates who have published their own books and shared their experiences with me about writing, including Ernie Hayden, Michael Lines, Marc Menninger, Matthew Webster, Kip Boyle, Sara Perrott, Bobby Rogers, Mike Eisenberg, and Dawn Dunkerley.

I'm grateful that Waterside Productions decided to publish this book. Thank you, William Gladstone, Josh Freel, and Maureen Maloney for your guidance.

Many thanks to Lisa Theobald, who served as both technical reviewer and copy editor. Lisa made numerous changes to the manuscript to improve its readability. Thanks also for feedback from Matt Webster, Mike Lines, Ernie Hayden, and Bobby Rogers. Gratitude to Madeleine Swart for expert and thorough proofreading.

Many thanks to my literary agent, Carole Jelen, for procuring writing opportunities over the past 15 years. Sincere thanks to Rebecca Steele, my business manager and publicist, for her long-term vision and for keeping me on track.

Despite having written more than 50 books, I have difficulty expressing my gratitude for my wife, Rebekah, for tolerating my frequent absences (in the home office while I developed the manuscript). I could not have completed this project without her loyal and unfailing support and encouragement.

PROLOGUE

About ten years into my professional career, I worked as a senior systems architect at World Vision United States, a Christian humanitarian organization in Monrovia, California. I had worked for many years as a software engineer, systems engineer, and security engineer on various operating systems, including CDC-6400 supercomputers, Unisys mainframes, DEC PDP-10 mainframes, DEC PDP-11 minicomputers, and—most importantly—Unix and C. I had designed and implemented relational database management systems and written C programs that manipulated data in those databases. I had plenty of experience at the detail level and the business level.

At World Vision, I designed information system architectures on Unix mainframes, specifically Sequent S27 and S81 Unix multiprocessor mainframes that ran the Informix Online RDBMS. I tended mainly to Unix systems architecture, network communications, data storage, and the Informix DBMS.

One of my colleagues at World Vision was an Informix employee named Liz Suto. Liz was a consultant to World Vision on the design, implementation, and operation of the Informix Online systems. About a year after I left my position at World Vision, Liz asked for my help. She was writing a book entitled *Informix Online Performance Tuning*, a technical book that helped Informix database administrators better understand how to anticipate and solve performance problems. Liz wanted me to be a technical editor for the book. My role would be that of a subject matter expert. After she had created the first draft of the book, I would review its contents to ensure two things: that everything in the book was factually correct, and that the way Liz explained things was appropriate and easy for readers to understand and follow. For this, I would receive compensation of a few hundred dollars, which, in 1994, wasn't too bad. I was being paid to learn and help Liz better explain new concepts to her readers.

This job was enlightening and enjoyable, and I was introduced to an executive at Prentice-Hall Publishing, a major publisher of technical books. I wrote to the executive, explaining that I enjoyed working on Liz's project, and expressed my interest in working on other projects if the publisher could use my help. I enclosed my resume. Over the next three or four years, Prentice-Hall sent me half a dozen book manuscripts for well-known technical books. Some of these books were published by Sun Microsystems Press, one of many vendor-specific labels for Prentice-Hall published books.

While performing these technical manuscript reviews, I was a consultant at McCaw Cellular Communications (which would later become AT&T Wireless) and wore many hats, including systems programmer, systems engineer, network engineer, and security engineer. I designed, implemented, and managed data networks and Solaris servers for business units with hundreds to thousands of employees.

In 1998, senior management put me in charge of IT architecture and engineering in a new, secret business unit at AT&T Wireless, where cybersecurity was extremely important. Being a Solaris shop (hundreds of engineering workstations running Pro Engineer, MATLAB, and several other tools), I believed it was essential to purchase a book on Solaris security to help me do a good job of ensuring the safety of our systems. Perusing Amazon.com and other online booksellers, I realized there were no books on the topic. I then had an epiphany.

I phoned the executive at Prentice-Hall, who was in charge of Sun Microsystems Press. The phone call went like this:

"Hi, this is Peter Gregory in Seattle."

"Hi Peter, how are things?"

"Pretty good. Say, I'm looking for a book on Solaris security, and find there is virtually nothing available. But you know what? I could write a book on Solaris security, since I already know a lot about the topic."

"Hey, Peter, that sounds like a great idea. Tell you what: please send me a table of contents, and I'll send you a contract that you can review and sign. How soon can you get started?"

There were almost certainly more words spoken in our conversation, but that is the gist of it. This was the only time I had to pitch a book idea to a publisher—a five-minute phone call.

We were in the heart of the dot-com boom, when anyone with a terrible business plan could get lots of seed money, or "angel money," as they called it. In my case, I was someone with a technical background who wanted to write a book that technologists building the technological gold rush would purchase.

I wrote the book, and after it was published, it was reasonably successful. Twenty years later, you can still buy a copy on Amazon.com.

Incidentally, I learned just a couple of years ago that every technical employee at Sun Microsystems received a copy of my first book, *Solaris Security*. I'm not sure whether this made any difference to me financially, but it was nice to hear that so many people owned a copy (in addition to the many thousands sold).

From then until now, I've written 51 manuscripts resulting in 56 published books (including this one). In every case, the publisher contacted me and asked if I would write the book. I've written perhaps four book proposals, mainly out of formality (because of my track record, the answer was usually yes).

My experience is not typical, however. I think my story is one of blind luck or Providence, depending upon your worldview. If a hundred of you readers are or will become published authors, I'm sure that no more than one or two of you have had or will have as easy a time as I did breaking into the business. In my case, it's more accurate to say the industry broke into me.

Most of you who become published authors will take a more typical path. Often this means you'll have a history of writing multiple articles for various magazines or technical journals, multi-part articles, and maybe even chapters of books written by many authors. It's not as easy getting into the publishing business today as it was for me more than 20 years ago. As Woody Allen once said, "Eighty percent of success in life is just showing up." I showed up at the right time in the publishing business, and I'm grateful for it.

INTRODUCTION

Many talented technologists who believe they have something to say to the world through published books don't know where or how to begin. Others want to be published but haven't developed a message. New avenues of publishing, such as e-books, provide choices that add to the unknowns.

If you're reading this book, you may be considering becoming an author of a technical book, or perhaps you've already written a manuscript and you're hoping to get it published. I hope the information provided here will help you embark on a successful journey toward becoming a published author.

Being a successful author requires that you possess several particular skills:

- The ability to understand a specific technology and to explain this understanding in both business and technical terms
- The ability to create a top-down structure for a complete book manuscript
- The ability to create book content that flows logically and is relatively free of grammatical, punctuation, and spelling errors
- The determination to stick to a long writing schedule and turn in chapters according to the schedule

- The fortitude to confront and overcome obstacles without losing sight of the goal
- The ability to work cooperatively with a team of book professionals to create the finished product

The idea of a new tech book begins with just that: an idea. Your first task, which may take days, weeks, or months to complete, is to develop the concept of the book and answer these questions:

- Who is the book's audience? Who are its intended readers?
- What is the book's objective?
- What "takeaways" should the book impart to its readers?

Next, it's essential that you determine whether any existing books are similar to the book you intend to write. To do that, you can perform a detailed analysis of your book idea, comparing it with similar books that have been published. Competition is not necessarily bad—in fact, it can be a good thing, because other books published on the same subject matter can serve to validate the demand for your book.

Then decide how you want your book to be published. If you're going to use a traditional book publisher, you'll need to write a proposal that sells your book idea to one or more prospective publishers. If you have a literary agent, this person may help you find a publisher that will publish your book. (I discuss literary agents in Chapter 1.)

Or, you may decide to self-publish. In this case, you will not need to "sell" your book idea to publishers, but you will instead publish your book as an e-book or with a "vanity publisher." While most of this book focuses on working with publishers, I discuss these options in this book as well.

The writing process is complicated and requires organization on your part in the form of detailed and complete records so that you know the status of every chapter and every image you will include in your book. At the peak of complexity, most tech book publishers expect you to continue writing later draft chapters while revising chapters that tech editors have reviewed, other chapters that copy editors have reviewed, and page proofs after compositors have completed their page layouts. This "publishing pipeline" can feel overwhelming, and without detailed records, you'll likely drop the ball somewhere along the line.

Even after your book has been published, there's plenty of work to do. After celebrating the completion of your book and experiencing the joy of unboxing the finished product, you'll need to begin promoting your book in various ways. Books don't promote themselves, after all, and most publishers generally do little more than place books on their websites.

Purpose of This Book

The purpose of this book is threefold: to open a window into the world of authoring, help you understand the writing lifestyle, and guide you in an organized way to succeed in your book project. If you have a book idea, you can use the guidance in Chapters 2 and 3 to create a book proposal to pitch to publishers. These chapters also provide information about the contract process and terms.

Many successful technologists have something valuable to share with the world, but few are familiar with the process of writing a full-length book. Fewer know how to work successfully with publishers, whether at the proposal stage or during the publishing process itself. It isn't easy to successfully market a book idea (even a good one), and the publishing process is complex. This book simplifies both so that you can get started on the writing.

During the past 25 years, I've written 51 full manuscripts (including this one), containing more than 12,000 pages and 3.6 million words. I have made plenty of mistakes; there were no books like this to guide me, so I had to improvise. Over the years, I have perfected numerous techniques that make my current book projects go much smoother than my earlier books. This book imparts these techniques to you.

You're free to use them and improve them further to suit your needs and the way you like to organize detailed work.

How This Book Is Organized

This book consists of information to help you take your tech book idea from concept to bound book. You'll find information about what it's like to be a writer, based on my experience.

There are seven chapters in this book, plus references and glossary sections:

Chapter 1: Before You Start A discussion of your book idea, why you want to write, and the writing lifestyle. Writing impacts your life, and I want you to know what you're getting into.

Chapter 2: The Book Proposal How to organize and develop a proposal that you'll send to publishers in hopes of getting a publishing contract.

Chapter 3: Legal and Logistics Various types of publishing channels, how to negotiate your contract, tips for researching information, and an introduction to the members of a publishing team.

Chapter 4: The Writing Process The process of writing the first draft of your manuscript, including setting up your writing tools and home office environment, organizing your chapter files and figures, understanding a publisher's content requirements, and understanding what to do if you need to alter your table of contents midstream.

Chapter 5: The Revision Process The twists and turns in the process of polishing your draft into a finished book. This chapter explains a typical publishing workflow and how to keep track of all the details, and you'll learn about the roles of the publishing team members.

Chapter 6: After Publication Your work is not done. Once your book is published, you need to promote it and generate sales. This chapter also shows you what to do when errors in the finished book are encountered.

Chapter 7: Writing Subsequent Editions Your book was successful enough that the publisher wants you to write the book's next edition. This chapter explains how this works in detail.

References and Resources A list of books and websites to consult to learn more about writing and publishing.

Glossary A list of industry-specific terms used by writers and publishers.

Although you can use this book as a reference and dive into any chapter, if you are a first-time writer, I urge you to read Chapters 1–3 before reading Chapter 4, particularly if your objective is to contract with a publishing house to publish your book. But even if you're going to self-publish, Chapters 1–3 provide valuable background information and essential truths that you need to know. Chapter 5 will get you familiar with the revision process required before your book goes to press. Once your book is published, Chapter 6 shows you how to get the word out.

1 BEFORE YOU START

When learning that I am a successful published author, many people I talk with tell me they want to write a book someday. Being a published author indeed carries some prestige, not unlike earning a college degree or climbing to the top of a well-known mountain. It is not easy to write any book, including a tech book or a textbook, and completing such an endeavor is a notable professional accomplishment.

Don't Start Writing Yet

Before you start writing, you need to accomplish a few tasks. If you haven't already started, don't start writing yet. Good things are worth the wait. If you have some thoughts and want to write them down, by all means, do that. Experience and wisdom come from learning from your mistakes. When you decide to author a book, your biggest mistake would be to begin doing so before creating a detailed plan.

Writing a tech book is a complex undertaking.

Early in my career, I was a programmer in early structured languages such as FORTRAN and C. When I was given a programming assignment, I was full of pent-up energy and would explode out of the starting blocks and begin writing code right away. Usually, I was coding right off the top of my head:

```
main(stdin, stdout)
{
int counter;
int flag1;
int flag2;
init(); {
```

...and so on.

It wouldn't take long for me to get lost—in my own code! Before I knew it, my program was more complex than I could imagine. So, I would examine my code, moving back and forth, to become familiar with what I had written so far. Then I could begin to build some structure to it. It was not a very happy experience, as I often felt defeated by my creativity.

A few years into my career, I took a university course in structured programming. We learned an analysis technique called Warnier-Orr, a methodology consisting of structured analysis and the development of a simple program design flow.

Not long after that, I was given a challenging programming assignment at work. I was to design and write a user-friendly text editor program for non-technical computer users. The basic requirements were to write a program that computer users would use to create or update simple text files. End users could insert lines, delete lines, and change the content of existing lines. This program's purpose was to enable people to edit a text file used to create a transaction report. The text file would specify the date range, search criteria, sort keys, and subtotal breaks.

Using the newly learned Warnier-Orr analysis technique, I designed the entire program on paper and worked out all the required logic. This step took me a few hours, and I worked on it until I knew I had it right.

I then transcribed this logic into source language (BASIC+ on PDP-11). I found one error in design, and after correcting that and a couple of typos, the program worked perfectly. Writing code from a completed design was a new experience for me. Creating a moderately complicated computer program from scratch and using my own design resulted in a program that worked properly and fulfilled its intended purpose.

This was an important life lesson, and it stuck with me. Henceforth, for any endeavor—whether I was writing a computer program or building something in my wood and metal shop—when I started from a complete design, the finished product turned out correctly, with few (if any) construction issues along the way.

My personal experience, learned at a relatively young age, compels me to advise you this: Your budding tech book project should begin with considerable planning. When executed, the plan will help you produce a better result that, overall, took you less effort than would be required if you simply inserted a sheet into your proverbial typewriter and started typing.

Consider the Writing Lifestyle

Writing a tech book takes a great deal of time. If you have a full-time job like I do, this means that you will likely have to stop spending time doing something else so that you can spend more time writing instead. Your choices for what to give up include, but are not limited to, the following:

- Spending time with your spouse or life partner
- Watching television
- Playing video or computer games
- Reading
- Exercising
- Engaging in hobbies
- Spending time with friends and family
- Cooking, cleaning, laundry, and yard work

- Taking vacations
- Sleeping

I've given up all the above—some permanently, others now and then. Foregoing each of these has a specific cost that you will have to consider carefully if you are thinking of writing a book. If you are careless with your choices, you could seriously impact your health and/or your most important personal relationships.

You probably won't make much money writing a tech book; it is up to you to decide whether the relatively minor monetary gain is worth the cost in other areas. What do you gain if you succeed in writing a book but lose your marriage, or you irreversibly damage your health? Don't write for the wrong reasons.

Being a Writer's Widow (or Widower)

As I write, Rebekah and I have been married for 16 years, and during those years, I have written more than 50 books. I would be beyond foolish if I claimed that my writing did not affect our marriage.

Time spent writing is time not spent in relationships. Allocating more time to writing comes with a high cost, and even the best marriage will suffer from neglect, even benign neglect, and even if your spouse or life partner supports your writing aspirations. I cannot put this more plainly.

I was already a writer when Rebekah and I met, so she had an idea of what she was getting into. Still, my time spent writing was, in retrospect, excessive. Perhaps my writing career is more successful as a result, but at what cost?

I have been fortunate, through no fault or doing of my own. Rebekah possesses a pioneer spirit, is resourceful and independent, and has a can-do attitude (with results) that few possess. Still, she has been justifiably resentful of my neglect. I cannot recount the number of vacations (including a cruise, and more than one weekend at our off-grid cabin) when I brought my laptop to work on a book.

I do now regret spending SO much "free time" writing. Although I cannot change the past, I changed my writing schedule, including no writing at all on weekends and no writing during vacations.

My advice to you is to consider the costs if you aspire to write. Discuss it with your spouse or partner before you start writing, as you write, and after you write. Be honest, count the costs, and decide whether it's worth it.

Know Why You Are Writing

Because you are reading this, you are at least flirting with the idea of writing a book. I applaud you for your aspiration. Writing and publishing a book is a significant accomplishment. I don't want to throw cold water on your enthusiasm, but I want to make sure you know what you're getting into and give you an idea of what the rewards *could* be.

If you are writing for money, that's fine. How much are you hoping to make from your writing project? I'll tell you from years of experience that it's improbable that you'll become wealthy from the proceeds of authoring a tech book, even one on a hot topic. For example, for an established author writing a promising title with a big publisher, an advance—the amount you receive after achieving a publishing contract—might amount to as little as $5000. Over the course of a year or two, if you're lucky, the book will "earn out" its advance (when book royalty earnings exceed the advance paid to the author), and you might make a little more money.

If you're not an established author, that advance could be as little as $1000—and consider yourself lucky, because publishers are a bit more risk-averse than they were in the dot-com boom of the 1990s. Back then, publishers offered larger advances on tech books on almost any topic (provided it had an Internet tie-in), but they got burned when the dot-com boom turned into the dot-com bust, and many of those book titles never earned out their advances.

Perhaps your interest in writing is for notoriety. Fair enough. If you manage to get your tech book published, you'll get your time slice of fame. What you do with it is up to you. If you are trying to become a big deal, publishing a book will advance your cause, even if just a little bit. If you have a big ego and you're trying to make it that much bigger, publishing a book may advance your cause. If attracting groupies is your idea of fun, then by all means, be my guest.

You are likely considering writing a tech book to advance your career. Being published is an accomplishment that will set you apart by demonstrating that you have the commitment, discipline, and drive to bring a big project to completion. That's a great message to impart to a current employer if you're vying for a promotion or to prospective employers if you're looking for something new (or at least someplace new).

Maybe you have a passion for helping people. Perhaps you believe that imparting your knowledge can help folks better understand how to use technology, and using your talent can help them understand what it means or how it can improve their lives or careers. If this is you, my hat's off to you: Having a passion for helping others is a higher cause—a noble cause, even. It suggests that you are not trying to improve your lot in life through writing, but instead, you want to help others. And if this is you, you're likely to be more successful for a few reasons. If you have a passion for helping others, this goal will serve as a driver to finish your project and to give it your very best all along the way. You'll earn more respect, too, because everyone loves a selfless hero. The same cannot be said for the narcissist or the egomaniac.

Define Your Book's Purpose

In addition to answering why you are writing, let's focus on the actual book again. Although this may seem like a pedantic question, it is crucial that you ask: What is your book's purpose? For a book to have value to a reader, it must have purpose.

I'll put this another way: What benefits will readers gain by reading your book? Will they learn something new about a particular topic? Will they understand how to perform some task? Will they think differently about something in their life? Will they experience some improvement in their profession or their personal life?

I'm suggesting that you ask these questions to make a point. Some aspiring authors think only of themselves and the benefits they will gain by writing a book. But self-actualization is an insufficient reason to write a book. By its very nature, a book is a form of communication from an individual (or, in the case of two or more co-authors, a small group) to a broader audience. If the book's publication benefits only its writers, then word will get around that the book's value for readers is low, resulting in disappointing sales figures. If this happens, your reputation with readers—and, more importantly, with the publisher—won't be so great, and the publisher may be reluctant to work with you again. Your first book will likely be your last.

Don't lose heart if you are unsure of your book's purpose. As you think about the book's subject and how you plan to write it, its purpose may become apparent.

If you are stuck, I suggest you look at some published books similar to the one you hope to write. Information on the front and back covers and the book's "Foreword" or "Introduction" should reveal its purpose and benefits to readers. By looking at other books in this way, you will begin to learn that books have an intended purpose. This concept should help you with your book ideas.

Your book's purpose will be closely tied to its intended audience, discussed in the next section.

Identify the Target Audience

Another essential characteristic of your book is its intended audience. In other words, who would benefit the most from reading your book?

Saying that "everyone" is a potential reader is a cop-out. Even bestselling authors such as Stephen King and J.K. Rowling know that their books are not truly for "everyone." Instead, the potential readers of your book fit one or more characteristics, such as these:

- Fit a particular age range, such as child, teen, young adult, middle-aged, or senior
- Inhabit a particular geography or a specific kind of place, such as a city, suburb, or small town, or live in a particular climate, country, or region
- Belong to a specific gender, ethnic group, people group, or language, political, spiritual, or religious affiliation or interest
- Work in a particular profession
- Have particular hobbies and interests
- Have a specific family situation or context, such as a parent, child, sibling, grandparent, married, single, divorced, cohabitating

If you are still struggling with understanding your target audience, I suggest you return to your book's purpose and subject matter. In your mind's eye, imagine who the readers of your book would be. What kind(s) of people would enjoy reading your book, and who would review your book in a positive light? It's also helpful to consider who would not necessarily want your book.

Knowing your audience is essential. If you hope to convince a publisher to publish your book, this is one of the first questions you'll be asked, and you must be confident in your answer. But even if you think you'll be self-publishing, it's essential to know your audience so that you can write a book that reaches the people you want to reach.

Define Your Book's Takeaways

Knowing your book's purpose and intended audience is not quite enough. One characteristic remains: your book's takeaways. In other words, what specific knowledge, skills, insights, or learning should your intended audience gain from the book and its purpose?

This question may feel repetitious, particularly after discussing your book's purpose. Instead, consider this a refinement of your book's purpose and audience. Maybe some examples of takeaways would be helpful to explain this concept:

- Understand how to select, set up, and use a Chromebook computer.
- Learn about the skills and knowledge required to pass the Certified Information Systems Auditor professional certification exam.
- Get familiar with many kinds of biometric technologies and how each works.

If you have not fully developed your book's purpose and audience, creating a list of takeaways is a great way to "drill down" into more details. Often, your takeaways will help you develop your book's structure and its table of contents, which is the subject of the next section.

Create a Table of Contents

Few individuals would construct a house without a blueprint, floor plans, and a bill of materials. Likewise, no tech book author should begin writing without first creating a fully developed table of contents (TOC).

Usually, before you begin writing the actual manuscript, you should finish the TOC. You'll need to have created a TOC before you pitch your book idea to a potential publisher. But before you develop your TOC, you should have identified your book's purpose, audience, and takeaways. At that point, the TOC should not be too challenging to create.

I'm not saying that developing your book's TOC will be easy! But without knowing your book's intended audience, purpose, and takeaways, building the TOC would be quite a difficult task. But have I told you, even once, that writing a book is easy? Far from it.

I suggest you begin by jotting down chapter titles, or even the names of the book's sections. Think of a TOC as an outline; in fact, that's precisely what it is! Even if you are a detail-oriented person, I suggest you get your chapter and section titles down first before you begin writing.

You'll read more about the importance of your TOC in book proposals in Chapter 2. Generally, you'll stick with this TOC as you write your manuscript. You'll also need to provide some page count estimates for your book chapters in your proposal, and you'll read more about this in Chapter 2 as well.

NOTE: I recommend you not begin writing chapter content until your entire top-level TOC is finished. Otherwise, you run the risk of having to rewrite some of that early content once you know what the rest of the book will include.

Develop Your Writing Technique

I suppose there is a rather romantic, prestigious, or sentimental notion associated with being a published author. Many writers want their name on a book, but few are up to the challenge. When you think you're ready to start writing, after you've completed all the things I suggested you do so far in this chapter, you still have some work to do before you begin.

Finding Your Voice

Every writer has a "writing voice." This voice is the author's writing style, the way they string words into sentences, sentences into paragraphs, and so on. "Tone" is another term used to describe the characteristics of writing. A writer's voice is like a singer's voice: each is distinctive and interesting, and some are more pleasant than others. To understand the appropriate writing style, and how to write using your unique voice, you need to consider the subject matter of your book, your audience, and your book's objectives.

Imagine that you are a classroom instructor, a mentor, or perhaps the reader's cool (and smart) friend, and you're helping the reader understand the technology that is the subject of your book—how the technology is used, mistakes to avoid, and so on. If you're having trouble figuring out what to say and how to say it, pretend you are in a personal setting and say it aloud. Listen to your words, and then write them down.

Remember that the people who buy your book want to understand the subject of the book—they may not understand the technology at all or may be looking for more information to help them better understand it. Your book must explain the big picture: how the technology works and how it is used, in plain language that is logical and makes sense. To a great extent, your success as a tech book writer depends on this skill and your voice.

Getting the Words Out

The book you're holding comprises about 43,000 words. Though this may seem like a lot of verbiage, it's a pretty small book compared to many others out there. Every book is written one word, one sentence, and one paragraph at a time. Quality is more important than size, although, of course, both are important.

Publishers don't care how fast you can type. That's your business, not theirs. Even though tech editors and copy editors will probably fix all your minor mistakes, publishers prefer to work with writers who can create good quality first draft copy according to the established schedule. This means that, although you don't need to produce perfect, error-free manuscripts, it is essential that you follow all the publisher's writing guidelines and write the best manuscript that you can.

How you decide to compose your book is a personal choice, from using a pencil or pen and paper (an unlikely scenario in this genre) to touch typing or using voice-to-text dictation.

Touch Typing

Knowing how to type without looking at the keyboard—touch typing—is beneficial for a writer, though it's not strictly required. If you must hunt and peck at the keyboard, your ideas may be obsolete by the time you get your draft completed! Speed itself is not the greatest virtue here, but even the fastest typists can "think" the words they want to type much faster than they can type them.

I first started typing at home on my parents' old Remington typewriter, which I still have today. I took a typing class in high school, working first on manual typewriters and then moving up to IBM Selectric typewriters. (This was in the age before most people had computers in their homes.) I'm a pretty good touch typist today and can type at a streak of about 90 words per minute if I'm typing long passages. A few years ago, I took a typing speed test, with the results shown in Figure 1.

Close Your Eyes

We're all writing on computers with word processors now. Sometimes, everything on the screen is a distraction. As you type, try closing your eyes. Don't worry about the mistakes—that's what autocorrect and spell checks are for. Just close your eyes and go, mainly if you are typing out a longer narrative and you're trying to type as fast as your thoughts come to you. Sometimes when you have a big idea, you'll start typing, but you may lose the entire thought before getting it all down. When you're not distracted by what you see on the screen as you type (such as autocorrect), you're more likely to be able to get the entirety of your thoughts on paper.

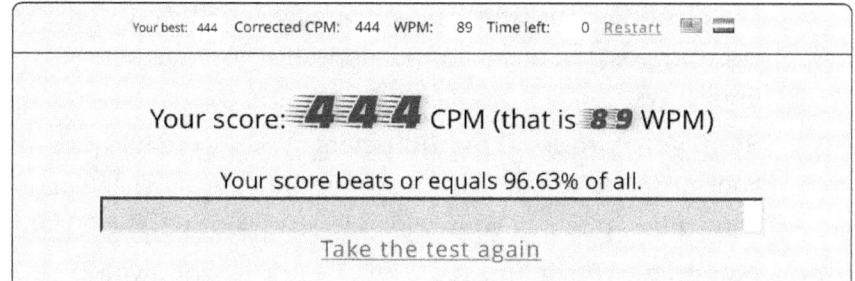

Figure 1. My typing speed test results from 2016 (source: author).

Voice Dictation

Voice-to-text dictation works well on today's computers. Microsoft Word and macOS have built-in dictation capabilities, and I've used both. It takes a bit of getting used to, but if you have a pretty good idea of what you want to say, dictation can help you get your thoughts onto paper very quickly.

You can also purchase software programs that will facilitate your dictation. Dragon Home is a well-known dictation program, but it's expensive ($200 for the consumer version, $500 for the pro version as of this writing), and it works only on Windows PCs. I have no experience with this or other programs, however.

Consider a Literary Agent

A literary agent is a publishing industry professional who represents author clients. Literary agents work on a commission basis and usually earn some percentage of your royalties—typically 15 percent. Getting an agent can be difficult, especially for a new author, because most literary agents receive far more requests from authors than they can reasonably take on. Most prefer to work with established authors who know the ropes. You can learn how to find an agent by doing some research online. Or, if you are friends with other authors, they may make agent recommendations.

If you are serious about writing books, an agent can help in several ways:

- **Help refine your proposal.** Your agent can help you refine your proposal to make it more appealing to potential publishers.
- **Shop your proposal to publishers.** Your agent will present your proposal to the right people in the right publishing companies, pitching your book idea and your writing talent.
- **Negotiate your contract.** Your agent will work with the publisher to get the best possible terms, including advance, royalties, rights, schedule, and other terms.

A few years after I started writing books, I hired a literary agent. This was the best decision I made in my writing career. My agent helped me acquire many authoring contracts at several publishing companies, which I could not have accomplished on my own.

2 THE BOOK PROPOSAL

Once you have determined your book's purpose, identified its target audience, established its takeaways, and decided how it will be organized, you're nearly ready to pitch your book idea to a publisher, or to a few publishers. Pitching a book project is entrepreneurship at its very best. You are a one-person business with a product idea, and you're looking for a company to build it for you. (I'll bet you didn't think you were in sales, but you are now! Congratulations and happy hunting!)

After you've written and delivered the draft manuscript, which costs you little or no cash to produce, a publisher will be paying staff (or freelance) editors, artists, designers, compositors, and printers to edit, design, lay out, and print your book. The publisher will also pitch your book to distributors and large retailers to stock and offer it for sale (though they won't necessarily help you market it to potential buyers). Do not be surprised to learn that your publisher will take approximately 90 percent of the gross proceeds of the sale of your book. After all, the organization has invested close to 100 percent of the cash in bringing your book to market.

If you think you'd rather self-publish and keep 100 percent of the proceeds, think again. Unfortunately, it's not quite so easy. For instance, unless you are a gifted tech editor, copy editor, illustrator, compositor, and proofreader, you'll be paying others to perform these tasks for you. And if you're going to be selling your books in hard copy, you'll have to pay a publisher or printer to print them. If you're selling e-books, of course, you can skip the printing part, but not the rest.

If you decide to self-publish, you also won't have a sales channel, so you'll have to work hard to get copies of your book on store shelves or at tech events—or you'll have to give up a good percentage of your proceeds to sell your book online through Amazon Kindle or other online publishers. If you compare self-publishing to having an actual publishing house publish your book, you will find you'll either get 10 percent of a potentially large amount of money or closer to 100 percent of a much smaller amount.

> **If Selling Is Uncomfortable**
>
> To be a writer is to be a self-promoter. You are a one-person business. The only way we survive as solo entrepreneurs survive is by "getting out there" and letting people know about our product so that readers can purchase it and add value to their personal or professional lives.
>
> If the idea of sales and self-promotion terrifies you, or you find it revolting, you have two choices:
>
> - **Power through it.** Perhaps you are like me, and staying forever in your comfort zone is ungratifying and lacks challenge. Confront your fears and face them head-on.
> - **Hire a literary agent.** An agent is your salesperson (and performs other helpful roles) in exchange for an agency fee, typically 15 percent of your royalties. You'll need to convince an agent that you are an author with reasonable chances of commercial success. For better or worse, you won't be able to avoid sales and self-promotion, but an agent can shoulder some of those burdens for you.

Although each publisher requires a particular format and structure for tech book proposals, the following are essential elements:

- Title or working title

- Author background
- Intended audience
- Purpose
- Market and competing titles
- Rights and copyrights
- Table of contents and page counts
- Illustrations
- Format
- Writing schedule
- Advance and royalties

Essentially, you are building a business plan for your book. Each of these elements is explained in detail in the remainder of this chapter.

Title or Working Title

Generally, your book's cover needs to display a title and perhaps a subtitle. While writing your proposal, you may or may not have decided upon your book's final title. If you are still working on this, you can refer to your book's title as a *working title*.

Even if you are firmly attached to a title, you should still consider it a working title in your proposal. For any of several reasons, a publisher that accepts your book proposal may have a different title in mind. If the publisher is willing to put up money to produce your book, its title should be the publisher's prerogative.

That said, the title of your book should not be a hill to die on. Suppose you appear to be intractable during the negotiation process. In that case, a potential publisher may take this as a sign that you are difficult to work with and may pass on your proposal altogether. Recall the old saying, "He who pays the fiddler calls the tune." An investor in a project will have some say in how the project will be run, and in this case, it includes your book's title and other elements of the book.

Author Background

The publisher needs to know about you and your abilities to ensure that you are the right person for the job. You need to convince them of several things:

- You are a subject matter expert on the topic of your book.
- You have a reputation as an expert on the topic.
- You have experience with similar projects.
- You can complete the work on time.
- They will like working with you.

Take any of these away, and most publishers will probably pass on your proposal. I'll explain further.

These days, publishers look for established and well-known experts on the topics to be covered. Many publishers won't give an author the time of day unless they already have some track record as a speaker at confabs or in webinars, an author of whitepapers or articles in journals, and the like.

As a prospective author, you must prove that you are an established expert. It is essential that you have demonstrable evidence of your expertise on the subject matter of your book to convince publishers that you are legitimately qualified to write about the topic and help persuade readers to buy your book. Without your having demonstrable expertise, such as having published several articles, teaching, or speaking at conferences, your book will not likely sell well. In the tech publishing industry, you sell books by being a known entity—and publishers want to be assured that your book will sell well! The publishing business is quite competitive, so readers are more likely to buy books written by established subject matter experts (SMEs).

Writing a full-length book is a complex and challenging undertaking, to put it lightly. Many would-be authors, star-struck by the prospect of being published, begin a project with enthusiasm but often give up when the going gets tough. And, believe me, it will get tough. Publishers considering investing in your book need the confidence that you will see the project through to the very end. Like most professionals, publishers highly value their time and prefer to spend time on projects that they are confident will be completed, and completed on time.

Publishers also need to be assured that you are technically capable of writing your book. Considerations include having a dedicated computer and software and a suitable writing environment.

Book projects are lengthy projects, often lasting from 3 to 12 months, and you'll constantly be interacting throughout the project with several different personnel in the publishing company. Publishers need to be confident that you can work cooperatively with a team. Life is too short to work with prima donnas and tyrants. Successful tech book authors are not superstars; they are team players. So, if you think that you will be running the show, think again. Many people on the team will know far more than you about the publishing process, and although you may be an SME on the book's topic, one or more of the book's tech editors may know even more than you do.

Multiple Authors

If you are writing your book with another author, or several others, you'll need to include all the information mentioned so far about the co-authors in your proposal. Additionally, you'll need to describe the division of labor among the co-authors. For instance, if you're proposing a book about information security, you may ask a cryptography expert to write the sections of the book that deal with that topic.

Another aspect of importance to publishers is writing consistency. For this reason, content written by two or more authors should be written in a similar style. You might think that having two or more authors makes for less work overall, but I hate to burst your bubble: there is potentially a good deal of work involved in making sure that the writing style—the author voice—of your book is as consistent as possible.

If you are the lead author of your book, one of your tasks will be to edit the draft manuscript(s) from your co-authors to ensure that the book is written and organized consistently. This can be quite a bit of work that you need to account for regarding the level of effort and schedule.

If you are considering subcontracting writing to co-authors, you must be upfront about this with the publisher. Often, your publishing contract will specify that you are the sole author and that you are not permitted to sub out your work. You'd best not violate this or any other term of your publishing contract, especially if you want your book to be published and you want to write more books in the future. Your publisher will need to consider many of the same aspects of authorship with any of your subcontractors—again, because they need to have confidence that the project will be completed on time and with the quality they expect.

Other Contributors

The bigger publishing houses will provide an artist, or illustrator, for your book—a professional who can render your scribbles into camera-ready art. Often, you will not be required to provide camera-ready art. If you want to specify who the artist will be, you'll need to be prepared to justify your preference, and that person's work will need to be evaluated and approved by the publisher.

You may also be thinking of bringing in your own tech editor. Although a publisher might let you do this, most publishers prefer to use one of their own tech reviewers. Publishers prefer to work with known, trusted parties, and they want to avoid the risk of a tech reviewer who thinks your manuscript is fantastic when, sadly, this may not be the case.

If you want to use your own trusted tech reviewer anyway, in addition to the publisher's tech editor, you will need to get the publisher's consent for this arrangement. The publisher may require that any other reviewers (your private subcontractors) sign a subcontractor agreement, which will define the owner of copyrights and other publishing rights, and require that the subcontractor comply with nondisclosure clauses. A subcontractor agreement will also determine matters such as payments and royalties. If your book is a big hit, the publisher doesn't want your subs suing for their "share" of the royalties.

It's likely that you will consult with one or more SMEs on various topics to make sure you have your facts straight. Though these other experts may not have a formal role in the book's creation, their contributions are nonetheless valuable, and you should at least recognize them in the "Acknowledgments" section of the book. You may choose to give them a signed copy of the published book.

Plagiarized Content

Three words: *Do not plagiarize.* Unless you've contracted with another writer to create content for your book (with your publisher's knowledge), or you have received explicit permission to use material written or created by someone else, you should *never* use content created by another person without attributing it to that author. And sometimes, particularly with copyrighted material, even that is not enough. It might seem like a harmless shortcut to cut and paste in some technical information written by another person from another book or publication, but be assured that this is often not okay without permission and credit, and it could result in you losing your book contract with your publisher, or worse.

Plagiarism is all too common in technical writing. Professional copy editors see it a lot, and they can sense its presence because the writing style suddenly changes. It may be a few sentences, a paragraph, or an entire section. Plagiarism is stealing, plain and simple. Please don't do it.

There are, however, some potential exceptions to this rule:
- For a passage up to a couple of sentences in length, you may quote and provide attribution for the passage.

- For a longer passage, you should obtain written permission from the copyright owner.
- If you are writing a book about a particular technology or product, you may be able to obtain permission to use longer passages and even entire sections. The terms of the permission you obtain will dictate whether you must provide attribution.

Publishers and authors are legally obligated to respect copyrighted material, and it is illegal to reprint copyrighted material without permission. For information on rights and copyrights, and to learn what content is free to use, see Chapter 3.

Intended Audience

Your proposal must be specific about the book's intended audience. Who are the most likely readers of your book? Think this through. Imagine that you are at a conference giving a talk on the book's subject matter and conversing with the people in the audience. Who are these people, and why are they here?

Here are some examples:

If your book is about…	*…your audience may be…*
New computational algorithms	Compiler or chip designers
Storage system management	System or database administrators
Chromebook computers	Nonprofessional computer users
Residential electrical wiring techniques	Homeowners, hobbyists, do-it-yourselfers
Advanced cat breeding techniques	Professional cat breeders

However, there is more to your intended audience than just who they are. You also need to know what your readers want to do. Here are some examples:

If your book is about…	*…your audience may be…*	*…who want to…*
New computational algorithms	Compiler or chip designers	Improve or enhance existing computer languages, create new computer languages, improve or design new computer chips

If your book is about...	...your audience may be...	...who want to...
Storage system management	System or database administrators	Improve storage system performance or manageability
Chromebook computers	Nonprofessional computer users	Learn how to use a new kind of computer
Residential electrical wiring techniques	Homeowners, hobbyists, do-it-yourselfers	Add more lighting or lighting features to their home, wire an addition to their home, wire a home they are building
Advanced cat breeding techniques	Professional cat breeders	Improve existing cat breeds, create a new cat breed

Purpose

A published book must have a purpose—a reason for existing. You, as the author, must know this as much as you know yourself. For your proposal to be successful, you must have passion for your book's purpose and must be able to convey this to the prospective publisher in concrete terms. What is a reader's desired result after reading your book? How is a reader changed by reading your book?

When I write professional certification study guides, I am writing for the following purposes:

- Help the reader understand the knowledge and experience required for a particular certification.
- Help the reader study for the certification exam.
- Help the reader understand how to maintain their certification.
- Help the reader know how to help others in their profession.

When I wrote *Chromebook For Dummies*, these were my objectives:
- Help the reader understand what a Chromebook is and how it differs from Windows and Mac computers.

- Help the reader select a Chromebook.
- Help the reader set up and use a Chromebook.
- Help the reader find helpful information about the Chromebook.

Another way to state your book's purpose in a proposal is to list a set of takeaways—benefits that the reader will obtain by reading your book. Here are some examples:

- Understand how to secure a web server.
- Understand how to select and set up a Chromebook and go online.
- Understand how to take better black-and-white photographs.

Market and Competing Titles

Before a publisher agrees to publish your tech book, you'll need to provide information about current trends and products that support your book's idea. There's no point in publishing a book with little or no reason to exist. The subject matter is probably related to something in the tech world that your potential readers will want to know more about.

The publisher will also want to know whether other books on the same, or similar, topic(s) have been published. This helps them better understand two things: whether the presence of other published books validates your book idea, and which books will be competing with yours.

Your proposal should include a list of three to six recent competing titles that are most similar to your proposed book. The information you need to incorporate about each title should consist of the following:

- Title
- Authors
- Publisher

- Year published
- Page count
- List price and/or price on Amazon.com (be sure to state which)
- Rating on Amazon.com (number of stars and number of reviews)
- A brief comparison of this book with your proposed book

Competing books offer value in addition to information for your proposal; they will likely provoke additional ideas about content to include in your book. Also, you may learn a bit more about the subject matter by reading competing books. To this end, I suggest you purchase and read some of the competing titles—you may find that you want to change your book somewhat. While I don't recommend you mimic the structure of competing books, you may be compelled to say more. You might even learn a few things you didn't know.

Before you include a book as a competing title, read all the reviews for each book, particularly any that have ideas you want to incorporate into your own. Reviews can help you ensure that you don't make the same mistakes made by other authors of similar titles. If, for example, there are errors in a competing title and other problems in how concepts are explained, you need to learn from those problems to avoid them in your book, lest you suffer negative reviews for the same reasons.

The absence of competing titles may indicate a lack of demand for books on this topic, or it could mean that your book presents a new and great idea about which no books have yet been published. Distinguishing between these two is vital to a publisher's decision to publish your book.

Shelf Life

Nonfiction books, by their nature, tend to reflect, describe, or propose ideas in culture, business, technology, and other aspects of life and living. Depending upon its subject matter, your book may be relevant for a finite period. For instance, *Who Moved My Cheese?*, a self-help book, may have a long shelf life, while *Sun Certified Systems Administrator for Solaris 8 Study Guide* (my second book) will be outdated far more quickly.

Publishers think about this. If they choose to invest in your book, they will need to build a business case for taking on your project. A crucial part of this is the number of copies the publisher expects to sell and how many years the book will generate sales.

Writers of tech books are keenly aware of this problem. Balancing relevance and shelf life is an art form at times. I have overcome this by discussing specifics (which often have a short shelf life) when needed and discussing concepts (which have a longer shelf life) when I can. Both are important, and the right blend of specifics and concepts will put your book in the "sweet spot" between relevance and durability.

A short shelf life is not necessarily a bad thing. If your book sells well and the underlying subject matter changes rapidly, you may be writing subsequent editions of the book. For tech writers, this can be the gift that keeps on giving. Chapter 7 discusses this topic in more detail.

Table of Contents

Your book's proposal must include a TOC, which is essentially the blueprint for the book that, at a high level, describes the flow and sequence of the story your book will tell. To invest in your project, publishers must have confidence that you are indeed an SME on the topic(s) in your book, and they also must have faith that you know how to tell a story that others will be willing to buy. The TOC tells the story at the macro level.

Readers often browse a book's TOC before deciding to buy it. The TOC reveals the book's structure; for a reader, it must be logical and appealing and tell the reader what the book includes. If the publisher judges that the TOC will appeal to readers, they will be more inclined to invest in your project.

Publishers require a list of chapters, but they sometimes want a TOC that includes "second-level" or even "third-level" headings. They want to see the major sections in each chapter, as well as the subsections. You might think that developing a TOC to this level of detail is a lot of work, and you'd be right! If you believe that you should not have to expend the effort of building out a fully developed three-level TOC for your proposal, you'll need to adjust your attitude. Even if you are a well-known writer and SME, publishers expect you to create a detailed TOC.

Your TOC also needs to include page count estimates. Specifying the estimated page counts for chapters is usually sufficient; you should not need to provide estimates for sections or subsections, though it might help you estimate each chapter's total length by adding up your estimates of each section's lengths. Usually, though, just the chapter page totals will suffice. Keep those other details to yourself.

A detailed TOC is a necessity; any publisher's acquisitions editor (the person who signs you to a book contract) will want to understand the detailed structure of your book before they consider investing in it. Think of it like this: If you were considering purchasing a home from a homebuilder, would you buy the home based on a few sketches, or would you want to see a complete set of blueprints showing all the details of the house?

A more detailed TOC demonstrates to a prospective publisher that you can build a more complex manuscript structure. Any publisher considering your book needs to have confidence in your ability to create a sound design, as well as a satisfactory manuscript.

If the publisher decides to publish your book, there is a possibility that, during the writing, you will be compelled to make minor adjustments to your TOC. I discuss this topic in Chapter 4.

Page Count Estimates

Publishers will ask you to provide page count estimates in your proposal for each chapter, plus the front matter (prologue, introduction, and so on), the back matter (charts and tables, lists, glossary, index, and so on), and other content. Before you can provide an accurate page count, however, you need to know the book's expected format—the height and width of its pages (aka "trim size"), the size of the margins and columns, and the typeface (aka "font") to be used. The book's publisher (or prospective publisher) should provide this information based on design specifications.

Some tech books include a list of tables and/or a list of illustrations at the back of the book (or sometimes at the front) that contribute to the page count. You and your publisher can determine whether these will be included in your finished book. In most cases, it is not necessary to develop this in advance.

Book Formats and Page Count Estimates

If you are submitting proposals to multiple publishers, it will help you to know the standard formats used by each publisher for their books, or a series of books. If you have an opportunity to learn about and view each publisher's book formats, you can tailor your proposals so that your page counts align with the formats they use.

Features of a publisher's book format can include the structure for a table of contents, copyright page, index, appendices, and other elements that are typically included. Your page counts can include or exclude these features; just be sure to specify whether they are included in your estimates. The format can also include the trim size of the book. One of my publishers, McGraw-Hill Education, uses a 7 1/4 in. by 9 in. trim format for books in its "All-In-One" series of study guides. Another, John Wiley & Sons, uses a 7 3/8 in. by 9 1/4 in. trim format for books in its "For Dummies" series. This book uses a 6 in. by 9 in. trim format.

NOTE: If you are accustomed to using footnotes in your writing, be sure your publisher's style guide permits them. Footnotes can be problematic in e-book formats.

Illustrations

Most tech books include illustrations and other graphical elements that help tell the story. As with the TOC and other aspects of your book, you should include an estimate of the numbers of each type of image you want to use.

Briefly, several types of images may be included in your book:

- Photographs, such as pictures of equipment
- Line art, such as hand-drawn schematics or flow charts
- Tables, such as device data or risk tables
- Screenshots, such as computer program windows or browsers showing a website

You'll need to estimate the number of lines (or portion of a page) that each of these elements will require, because they contribute to your total page count.

Your proposal should also include information about the nature of the images that will appear in your book, as well as their origins. (For information on rights and copyrights, see Chapter 3.)

Publishers can accept line art in two forms: rough draft line drawings, or sketches, that artists will be rendering into finished line art; or camera-ready line art, digital documents that are ready to be printed. If your book includes several illustrations, you'll need to specify this, because rendering rough sketches into camera-ready art can be time-consuming and expensive. Chances are you won't be submitting camera-ready art. Most authors are not technically proficient in producing camera-ready art; publishers' requirements for digital art involve many techniques that are well-known by professional artists but not by tech book authors. You'll need to know each publisher's standards for submissions of photographs, screenshots, and line art to determine what you'll be required to provide. For instance, publishers generally require black-and-white images with a minimum dpi (dots per inch—for quality).

Format

Your proposal will cite the format you'll use to write your book. Today, most publishers use Microsoft Word in its native XML format, with liberal use of the Track Changes feature as tech editors and copy editors make corrections in the process.

Many publishers distribute a book template file and writing style guide to authors. Your proposal should cite that you will accept and use any template and style guide to express your willingness to collaborate using the publisher's established toolset.

It is not wise to insist that you will deliver your manuscript using a word processor that the publisher does not support natively (for example, you want to use Google Docs or another word processor instead of MS Word). If you insist on using a different word processor, you are telling the publisher, "I do not play well with others." If you want to do business with a publisher, you must use their toolset and comply with their requirements.

Writing Schedule

Your proposal needs to include a writing schedule. Mainly, the publisher needs to know how soon you will produce the rough draft, and whether you will deliver each chapter as it is completed or submit the entire draft manuscript at once. Tech publishers generally prefer to receive each chapter as it is written so that tech editors and copy editors can get to work on early chapters while you write later ones. Overall, this results in the entire book being completed quickly. In tech publishing, time is of the essence, especially for books concerning new technology. Your publisher wants to be the first to market to sell more books than the competition.

Publishers I have worked with don't like writing schedules that extend longer than six months. The reasons for this are financial and involve scheduling logistics for tech editors, copy editors, printing, and other aspects of publishing.

Advances and Royalties

A book proposal does not need to discuss advances and royalties, because the publisher will propose an advance and royalty schedule that is competitive but not too risky. If you are an experienced writer with several books under your belt or have a good literary agent, you may be in a stronger position to suggest terms.

Remember this: Publishers are not trying to drive your royalty percentages to the lowest possible level. Publishers compete with one another, including competing to attract talented authors. If you are an author with good credentials and a solid book proposal, each publisher will expect that you are shopping your proposal to several publishers to look for the best deal.

Confidentiality

You can be sure that any publisher that receives your book proposal will keep it confidential. Although it's wise to include a copyright declaration with your proposal, and perhaps a confidentiality word or phrase, the publisher will not misuse your proposal—they won't steal your idea and give it to another author, for instance.

Demanding that a publisher sign a nondisclosure agreement (NDA) is a bit heavy-handed. Still, it would be reasonable to ask a publisher if they have a bilateral or reciprocal NDA that you could sign. Just know that the publisher first needs to determine whether you are someone worth dealing with. If you are proposing *Cold Fusion at Home For Dummies* or something equally compelling, you might have a case for an NDA, but most authors are not in a position to demand one. When you're just starting out in writing, you must play by the publisher's rules. If you have an agent, your agent can advise you of the particulars.

Circulating Your Proposal

After submitting your proposal to a publisher, it will likely be circulated internally to various acquisition editors and staff members. It's also possible that they will send the proposal to trusted outsiders (often tech editors and authors they already work with) to get their opinions. Any publisher wants to establish a consensus on whether to invest in a book. Note the word "invest." Remember that a publisher will be putting up a lot of soft and hard dollars to publish your book. If they give you a book contract, they make a financial bet that your book will be profitable. Because they want the odds of that bet to pay off, they may first seek others' opinions of your proposal before they commit.

3 LEGAL AND LOGISTICS

Much legal and logistical business is involved in producing a book, whether an agent represents you or you are on your own, and whether you work with a publisher or self-publish. You will have legal agreements to read, negotiate, and sign. Various publishing channels are available to you, each with pros and cons.

This book assumes that you will be working with a publisher, where you'll be part of a team of professionals with various skills and roles. Succeeding in your writing project requires you to understand these roles and how they contribute to your book's completion.

Publication Channels

When I started writing books in the 1990s, there were only two ways to get your book published: pay a publisher to publish your work, or find a publisher that would pay you to write your book. Today, numerous self-publishing platforms provide many more choices and opportunities to get your published work into the marketplace.

Still, in my opinion, the Holy Grail is the publishing house that will pay you to write your book, including a cash advance. However, the path leading to this traditional publishing method may include self-published e-books.

Vanity Publishing

I hope that you will avoid the option of paying a publisher to publish your book. Known as "vanity publishers," these companies will publish anything and everything, and you'll pay for it all, including the boxes of finished books shipped to your door. Marketing, distribution, and sales are all up to you in this arrangement. If you have a day job, you probably don't have time to do any of these things, and to be successful, you'll need to be experienced at all of them. Otherwise, it's unlikely that you'll earn back what you had to pay the publisher.

Self-Publishing

Self-publishing is the new kid on the publishing block. You write your book and upload it to the self-publishing platform you have chosen, and *voila*! Your book is published and for sale to readers in electronic form. Amazon's Kindle Direct Publishing (KDP) is the king of the hill in this business.

Amazon pays you a higher royalty percentage than a traditional publisher, but there's a catch: you must develop all the content yourself. If you want tech editors, copy editors, and artists to review and improve your work and create images for the book, it's up to you to make those arrangements and pay those professionals as you develop the manuscript. You could say that KDP is a kind of vanity press; however, your finished book will be made available for sale on Amazon.com. If your book is good, you'll get good reviews, and you may be able to sell many copies.

One more thing about KDP: Read the contract carefully, as KDP may impose an *exclusivity requirement*, meaning that for some time (one year, last I checked), you cannot publish or sell your book on any other platform.

Other good platforms for publishing e-books include Smashwords, Lulu, Barnes & Noble, Leanpub, Reedsy, Ulysses, and Scribd.

Negotiating Your Contract

If you are in the fortunate position of having a legitimate publisher agree to publish your book, your conversation with the publisher has pivoted from "Will you publish my book?" to "Under what terms and conditions will you publish my book?"

There are many critical points to find and carefully read in your contract, with details too numerous to mention. The high points, however, are rights, royalties, remedies, and a bit more.

This section offers abbreviated descriptions of all the information you need for negotiating your contract. If you have a literary agent, they will represent you and get you the best possible terms. If you are publishing through Amazon Kindle or other e-book channels, the terms are likely non-negotiable unless you are a best-selling author like Stephen King, in which case you'll get special treatment. The rest of us, including tech book writers, won't be so lucky.

Whether an agent represents you or not, I suggest you pick up a copy of *How to Be Your Own Literary Agent: An Insider's Guide to Getting Your Book Published*, by Richard Curtis. This book explores the nooks and crannies of book contracts and other aspects of publishing that, as a writer, you ought to become familiar with.

The parts of the contract you should be most familiar with are discussed in the following sections.

Manuscript Preparation

You must agree to write the book on the agreed-upon topic, in a certain number of pages, and by a specific time. You may see statements about the quality of the manuscript. The contract should specify who supplies photographs and illustrations, who creates the index, and who pays for these and other things.

Your book's TOC may be a part of the contract, as a way of holding you to writing your book according to the structure outlined therein.

The contract will require you, as the author, to guarantee that you will not plagiarize any content in the preparation of your manuscript or in the use of any illustration.

Co-authors

If you are writing the book with one or more co-authors, the contract will state all the authors' names and the sequence of their names on the cover and elsewhere. The contract will stipulate the percentage of proceeds the publisher will pay to each author.

Rights

Your contract will state who owns the copyright for your book. Simply put, if the publisher owns the copyright, the finished work content is the publisher's property to publish in any way they choose. You cannot sell or give away the book or have it published by another publisher if you are unsatisfied with the results. The book and its content belong to the publisher, and you sold it to them.

If you own the copyright to your book, the book's content is your property. Still, with a publishing agreement, you may be agreeing to give the publisher exclusive rights to distribute and sell your book, perhaps for a specific period, after which you are permitted to publish elsewhere or self-publish.

The contract may require you to list all the sources of content created by others, including written material and images, that will be included in your book. It may even require you to obtain permission from the owners of these. Generally, the publisher will not agree to make payments to the owners of these items unless one or more of them is of paramount importance in your book. However, the publisher may agree to pay a modest sum for an image to be used on the cover.

As the author, you will agree not to publish or self-publish any work that appears to compete with the book you will write. In other words, if you are unsatisfied with your book or your publisher's effort to sell it, you cannot write the same or a similar book and publish it through another publisher (or self-publish).

Royalties

Royalties are the proceeds you receive when copies of your book are sold. Your publishing contract specifies royalties as a percentage of the retail price, the wholesale price, or other prices set for your book. There will often be several different rates for your book sales through various sales channels. For instance, book club sales rates may be lower because the publisher sells to the book club in bulk at a discount. Other channels include international sales, e-books, direct marketing, translations, and subsidiary rights (which cover every form of the book that is not the physical book itself).

The contract will specify the schedule of royalty payments. Typically, royalties are paid quarterly, semi-annually, or annually. Your royalty statements will include a detailed accounting of the number of copies sold through each sales channel.

A typical royalty percentage might range anywhere from 6 percent to 15 percent; 6 percent would be considered low, but if you have never published a book before, chances are the publisher will pay royalties on the low side because you are unproven talent. Plus, it may take more than the usual level of effort to publish your book, and your book may not be altogether successful. Generally, the greater the publisher's risk, the lower the royalty percentage. But on the high side, I would say that anything greater than 11 percent is generous. This rate may seem a measly amount, but remember that the publisher has numerous employees, contract staff, and investments in manufacturing and distribution that are all a part of publishing your book. You are just one of many persons required to take your book from a draft manuscript to a finished, manufactured product on the shelves of thousands of bookstores and online sales warehouses.

Publishing contracts often stair-step royalties. For example, your contract might specify a 10 percent royalty for the first 10,000 copies sold, followed by a 12 percent royalty when more than 10,000 copies are sold. This scheme is an incentive for you and the publisher to produce quality work that will sell more copies and encourage you to promote your book.

Advance

Your contract may include a mention of an "advance," which is an advance payment of anticipated royalties. The advance may be a single cash payment or multiple payments, each tied to specific milestones. For instance, you may receive an advance when you submit the first completed chapter, another when you have completed 50 percent of the draft manuscript, and another final payment when you have completed the entire draft manuscript.

New authors sometimes forget that an advance is money subtracted from future royalties. For example, suppose your contract pays you a $1000 advance, and when your book is published, the royalties will be $2 per copy sold. The royalties from the sale of the first 500 copies of your book will pay back the advance, after which the publisher will pay you directly. When your book's royalties have entirely paid back all advance payments, the book is said to have "earned out" its advance.

Another way to think of a royalty payment is to consider it a payday loan against future earnings.

Basket Accounting

Publishers often use a technique known as "basket accounting," whereby publishers use royalties from a successful book to pay back the advance for a less successful book. For example, suppose you write a book on Cisco routers; you receive a $5000 advance, but the book does not earn out its advance. Later, you publish another book at the same publisher on Linux servers. In basket accounting, the Linux servers book's royalties will have to earn out for both the Linux servers book and the Cisco routers book before you receive any cash royalties.

Basket accounting is a publisher's way of recouping losses from unsuccessful books. Although you probably won't be able to prevent this practice altogether, you may be able to limit it. A good literary agent can help you with this kind of issue.

Author Personal Copies

When publishing a typical paperback, softbound, or hardbound book, you'll want the publisher to set aside 6 to 12 copies that they'll ship to you when the book is published. The publisher will pay for shipping. You may be forbidden from selling these copies; however, you'll have other uses for them, as I discuss in Chapter 6.

If your book is being published only as an e-book, you should be given a similar number of free-copy codes that you can give away as gifts.

Information Sources

Technical books rely on a considerable amount of information gathered from many places. The business of writing requires that you carefully track all the sources you use. For your sanity, you should also track all the resources you looked at but didn't use, because later in your project, for example, you might want to refer to that blog article you read and initially thought was of little value. This research may take considerable time, and you don't want to rely solely on your memory when you need to use it.

Keeping Records

As a writer, you must keep thorough, detailed records of all your sources of information. Failure to do so will, at best, result in much wasted time and, at worst, result in legal trouble.

Most technical book authors rely upon a considerable amount of information obtained from official and unofficial sources. As you write, I suggest you also have a document or worksheet open where you record all the books, websites, and other sources you consult during your research, whether you use information from them or not. You may be looking for a particular technique and run across an insightful corporate or professional blog article, even if you don't use that information in your book. If you don't record this, you might find yourself later scurrying through your browser history in a desperate search for that one nugget that you now consider essential.

In my books, I tend to use numerous photographs and illustrations that were initially published elsewhere. As I discuss in detail in Chapter 4, you've got to keep a complete attribution record every time you grab an image you are considering using in your book. If you decide to include an image created by another party in your book, you must thoroughly explore and understand the copyright terms to avoid getting into legal trouble later.

Tracking Permissions

When you include images in your book that come from websites or other sources, you'll need explicit permission to use them. Often, you're responsible for doing the hard work of determining the owner of an image and then writing to them, explaining what you want to do with their image, and then collecting and saving their consent.

You'll also need to negotiate the attribution to be used. In other words, when you use an illustration that is the property of another, you need to mention it in the associated caption or an "Image Credits" section in your book. For instance, an image caption might include words such as "Image courtesy of Kodak Corporation."

Your publisher may request that you provide evidence of permission for one or more of the images used in your book. As the entity with deeper pockets, it is more likely that a copyright owner will sue a publisher if an image is used without permission. In such a circumstance, you will also be in serious trouble. Dishonesty and sloppiness are career killers.

Manufacturer-Provided Details

Often, when you're writing a tech book about a product, you'll be obtaining information from the product's manufacturer. At times, you may be receiving non-public or prerelease information from a manufacturer about the product that is the topic of your book. For instance, if you are writing a book on the next version of a popular smartphone operating system, the manufacturer may provide you with details of new features. It is essential that you keep this information so that your book will include it and thus be considered current. However, you must also agree not to share any of those details in any other way.

Often, you will be asked to sign an NDA by the product manufacturer. Because you are one of three parties (the manufacturer, the publisher, and you) who are privy to confidential information, all three parties may be required to sign the agreement, or there may be separate NDAs for you and the publisher.

Subject Matter Experts

The chances are good that, at some point in your book project, you'll need to consult with someone who has more knowledge than you about a particular subject. Perhaps this SME is a co-worker or business associate. Regardless, it's common to do a little fact-checking during your project by checking with SMEs. Be sure to record these contacts in your records with enough detail so that you can backtrack later on if needed. You'll also want to consider publicly acknowledging your SMEs in the "Acknowledgments" section of your book as a way of thanking them for their assistance.

Copyrights

As an author, it is vital that you understand the basics of copyright law. I'll give it to you in a nutshell: You cannot appropriate the works of others in the work you assemble to sell for a profit. If you do, there will be consequences in the form of cease-and-desist orders and lawsuits. Of course, it is not as simple as that, but that's the root concept. The creators of content are, for the most part, the owners of that content, and it is their property according to copyright law.

Manuscript Rights

When you negotiate the contract for your book, one of the most critical sections of the agreement that you must understand describes the ownership of the content you write. Although common sense would tell you that you would be the owner as the creator of your book's content, this is often not the case. In many publishing companies, the publisher owns the rights to your finished work. Before you cry foul, understand that this is simply a part of the transaction. When the publisher has exclusive rights to the content, they will be free to market and sell your content in many forms through many channels. If you own the rights to your book, you and the publisher may become competitors in the marketplace, and the relationship between you and the publisher could become adversarial; in my opinion, this is not a good writer-publisher relationship. Let your publishers have the rights and make as much money as possible from your book, and remember that you will get your cut.

Better publishers are pragmatic on this topic. For instance, many publishers will permit you to give away a free chapter as a part of your book's promotion. In this regard, the publisher will even help you by packaging your free chapter in a professional PDF or e-book format. Publishers may also permit you to publish excerpts. Before you proceed, however, I recommend you check with them to be sure they will allow it. For instance, I often publish paragraphs of draft manuscripts as a part of a blog or professional social media postings.

Using Copyrighted Work in Your Book

Earlier, I mentioned the need to keep detailed records of excerpts and images you use in the book. This is all a part of working with and understanding copyrights. The creators of images and other content often cite the terms by which others, including you, may use that content in some sort of a transaction. You may be required to provide attribution, and sometimes you may need to compensate the creator. (I have never had to do this, although a few of my books include cover images that were purchased.)

You can include short written passages from other published works in your book. However, in addition to putting that passage in quotation marks or offsetting it in some other way, you should include an attribution. My own rule of thumb is that a paragraph is the most that I would ever want to borrow from another work to include in my own. And if I do include it, I am always sure to attribute it to the author.

Public Domain Content

A considerable amount of content is said to reside "in the public domain"—that is, no exclusive intellectual property rights apply, and you're free to use it. However, this does not mean that you should appropriate it and claim it as your own. Attributions are still necessary.

In addition, as you look for images for your book, know this: Photographs taken by U.S. government employees while on the job are considered public domain. This also includes images that appear on U.S. government websites unless, of course, a specific attribution stipulates that another party owns an image.

One of my favorite sources for images is the nonprofit Wikimedia Commons. Most images on their website have copyright terms that permit you to use the images in your book, although you are usually required to provide attribution.

Content from Manufacturers

If you are writing a technical book, you'll often include images of products or diagrams that you obtained from product manufacturers. Frequently, manufacturers are pleased to have their products depicted in a book—but, again, it's crucial that you provide attribution. In some instances, you'll want to include a passage from a technical manual or product description in your book. These excerpts should also be clearly indicated and attributed to a specific publication.

Recordkeeping

When you need to obtain permissions to use images, keep detailed records for each image, including archiving e-mail correspondence. I suggest making PDFs of specific messages granting permissions and saving those in your records. Your publisher may require that you forward them these e-mail messages to maintain their own paper trail.

Chapter 4 discusses recordkeeping in more detail.

NOTE: You need to be familiar with your publisher's policies on using copyrighted material and attributions in your book. Different publishers take slightly different approaches according to their risk appetite and other considerations. Be sure you completely understand your publisher's requirements for recordkeeping, including obtaining permissions for including content owned by other parties.

The Team

Publishing a book is a team sport, and you are the star player. However, you've got to be a team player and not a prima donna, or your publishing career will be a brief one. You'll be more successful if you consider yourself a member of a team of experts, and the other team members will enjoy working with you more than if you consider yourself the smartest person in the room.

Note that all publishing team members work on multiple book projects simultaneously, including yours. Do not consider them resources dedicated to your project only.

The team members on your book project will include the following:

- Author
- Co-author(s)
- Acquisitions editor
- Project editor
- Technical editor
- Copy editor
- Artist
- Proofreader
- Designer
- Compositor
- Indexer
- Manufacturing staff
- Distribution staff
- Marketing staff
- Merchandising staff
- Sales staff

Author

The author is you—the person who develops the book's TOC and who writes the manuscript's draft. As discussed earlier in this chapter, the author and publisher enter into a legal agreement. The author promises to write the entire draft manuscript within a set time, and then works through detailed feedback from project editors, tech editors, copy editors, and proofreaders.

The author is also responsible for creating and/or acquiring any images that appear in the book. For images owned by others, the author is responsible for understanding each one's copyright terms and conditions, obtaining permission from the copyright owner to use the image(s) in the book, and understanding and creating all necessary attributions (such as photo credits).

Co-author(s)

You may write a book in tandem with one or more authors who share the writing of the first draft and reviewing subsequent drafts of portions of the book. Sometimes the division of labor is outlined in the contract, but often these details are up to you. Usually, the acquisitions editor will be familiar with who is producing what content and the development workflow if two or more authors review other authors' work. You and your co-authors are generally the only members on the project team who do not work for the publisher as employees or contractors.

Acquisitions Editor

The acquisitions editor (AE) is the publisher's representative responsible for acquiring authors and developing content for books. You'll work with the AE to negotiate your book contract with the publisher, and some AEs review and develop the content of newly acquired books, making suggestions to the author. The AE is usually your first contact at the publishing house. This person, along with the project editor, will serve as your main point person throughout the project, particularly if problems occur. However, in some publishing houses, the AE may be a "behind the scenes" player you won't deal with very much throughout the project.

Team members don't report directly to the AE in a larger publishing company. Instead, teams report to the managers of their various departments, but the AE serves as the ultimate leader of the book project. The AE is also the person who is consulted when an author underperforms or causes delays in the writing schedule. The AE is answerable to the publisher and regularly reports on ongoing book projects, including yours.

Project Editor

The project editor (PE) is usually, but not always, an employee of the publishing company. The PE manages, or co-manages, the production details of your book project, from editing through page proofs. Generally, you'll be sending and receiving chapter files directly to and from the PE, who will manage the team of workers who edit and produce the book. The PE tracks the movement of every chapter file and other artifacts such as images. However, this does not mean that you don't need to do your own detailed recordkeeping. For more on recordkeeping, see Chapter 4.

The PE may include the AE in correspondence with you, and vice versa. In smaller publishing companies, the same person may serve as both the AE and the PE.

Technical Editor

Tech editors (TEs) are SMEs familiar with the topics discussed in your book. These TEs aren't necessarily authors themselves, but they are known for having expertise in one or more subjects and are skilled at recognizing and correcting technical narratives for correctness and readability.

A TE is rarely a publisher's employee but is usually employed elsewhere and participating in a book project as a subcontractor. Bigger publishing houses have an extensive portfolio of SMEs on a wide variety of subjects. Often, the publisher will select the TE, but some publishers will rely on a trusted author to recommend TEs from their own list of contacts. The publisher will enter into a legal agreement with the TE (to clarify non-disclosure and intellectual property ownership) that is similar to agreements created with other subcontractors.

TEs are tasked with reviewing and editing electronic manuscripts and tracking their edits and suggestions (using Track Changes if the manuscript is in MS Word). They carefully check descriptions, explanations, and techniques described in your book, and then make necessary corrections or suggestions. TEs are not responsible for making corrections such as spelling, grammar, punctuation, or style, except in cases where copy editors and proofreaders, who are not SMEs, would not make such corrections.

Generally, AEs or PEs send first draft chapters to TEs, who make corrections and insert comments (often questions or suggestions) directly into the draft manuscript. Then the author is asked to review the TE's changes and comments before updating the manuscript and resubmitting it to the PE.

If the publisher permits you to select your book's TE, ensure that the TE understands the time commitment. The TE cannot merely skim the content to watch for obvious errors that leap off the page; instead, they must read every paragraph slowly and critically. You count on the TE to suggest better ways of explaining concepts and procedures, correct mistakes, and suggest additional content. My advice is to let the publisher select the TE, but make sure you know that this person is qualified for the role. If you choose the TE, be sure that your relationship is one of respect so that the relationship will not be damaged if and when the TE appears overly critical of your work. If your TE is afraid to say what needs to be said for fear of damaging the relationship, perhaps you should look for someone else to do the review.

My publishing career began as a TE for the book *Informix Online Performance Tuning* in the mid-1990s. In those days, a TE was shipped a printed copy of the draft manuscript and was expected to use traditional proofreading marks in pencil before shipping the manuscript back to the publisher. I was a TE for several titles before writing my first book, *Solaris Security*, in the late 1990s. The TE experience provided some insights that helped me write that first book, plus all those that followed.

Copy Editor

The copy editor (CE) is an SME in language and technical and expository writing. The CE's job is to examine sentence structure, spelling, punctuation, tone, tense, style, paragraph structure, consistency, and the manuscript's flow of explanations and descriptions. They also check references within the book, including websites and other publications that are mentioned. Although CEs are not usually SMEs on the specific technology being discussed, they should be experienced in how various classes and types of technologies are described and explained. It should be no surprise that experienced tech CEs know a bit about many topics after poring through many book manuscripts.

Like TEs, CEs usually track their edits (often using Track Changes in MS Word) so that authors will be able to see and evaluate all their changes. CEs often insert notes into the manuscript, asking the author to make specific corrections that only the author is qualified to make. For instance, a CE may recognize that a passage does not clearly explain a concept or procedure and ask the author to rewrite it in some specific way. Occasionally, a CE will take a stab at it and ask the author to validate and refine the change.

Good CEs improve technical manuscripts by making them easier for readers to read and understand, and by making sure the book is written consistently and predictably.

Artist

Larger publishers use staff or freelance artists or illustrators who render an author's scribbles or sketches into camera-ready line art. In some instances, publishers will require authors to create camera-ready illustrations, or drafts drawn with Visio, PowerPoint, and other tools that artists will touch up and finalize.

Because an illustrator's work takes time, an author's writing contract may limit the number of images they will render for a book project. Exceeding this number may require that the author forego a portion of their advance or select which illustrations can be omitted.

Artists may manipulate photographs to make them appear satisfactorily on printed (or electronic) book pages. This manipulation may involve cropping, adjusting brightness and contrast, changing resolution, and converting color to black and white. Sometimes, an artist will find that a particular photograph will not render well in the book (often because of low resolution) and request a better or different image.

Designer

The book's designer creates the book's cover and designs the internal pages of the published book. The designer selects the typefaces (fonts), the physical (trim) size, the overall page layout, and sometimes the paper used inside the book and its binding. This person also designs elements such as headings, sidebars, special notes, charts, graphs, artwork, and various other visual components of the book.

Compositor

Compositors perform page layout for the manuscript using specialized design software, such as Adobe FrameMaker. They control font spacing, margins, text flows, page breaks, and the placement of illustrations and tables. Compositors format photos and line art provided by the author and/or artists and position them, along with captions, on pages.

The job of composition may appear straightforward, but the work involves numerous challenges. The text on each page needs to appear in neat, consistent blocks. Compositors look out for and avoid instances of "widows" (which occur when the last line of a paragraph from one page appears at the top of the next page) and "orphans" (which occur when the first line of a paragraph appears alone at the bottom of a page), as well as section headings orphaned at the bottom of pages.

Compositors lay out tables, avoid unsightly page breaks where possible, and sometimes turn an illustration or table 90 degrees to fit on a page. The placement of images and tables with their respective captions requires some skill. They should not appear too early (before being referenced in the text) or too late (appearing within the next section or subtopic).

Finally, compositors strive for an efficient book layout—not stretching, but compacting the text so that the book fills as few pages as possible, without the text and artwork appearing too tight or crowded.

The finished book layout is encapsulated in the book's page proofs, which are the camera-ready page layouts ready to be sent to the printer. Page proofs are usually sent to the PE, the proofreader, the author, and the indexer for further scrutiny before they go to press. Like a beautiful poem, painting, photograph, or product design, the compositor's final product is elegant, but it rarely reveals the significant amount of work involved.

Proofreader

Proofreaders give the manuscript one final read-through after the compositor has created page proofs; they examine many details to ensure that no mistakes appear in the printed book. The proofreader is one of the last sets of eyes to scrutinize the manuscript to find and correct any issues before the book goes to print.

A proofreader checks the page proofs electronically as PDF documents or in printed form for grammar and spelling concerns missed by other reviewers. Proofreaders also: ensure that page numbering is correctly sequenced; check headers and footers; check margin alignment, text alignment, and format; and focus on other details. At this point, the indexer also works on a copy of the page proofs, and the author is asked to review the page proofs at the same time. This is also the author's last chance to make any necessary corrections. The publisher usually allows limited issues to be corrected at this stage, because it can be expensive, both in time and money, to send the book back to the compositor, especially if the schedule is tight.

Once the proofreader has completed their work and the author has signed off on the page layouts, the PE compiles the corrections and sends them back to the compositor. The final pages, corrected and camera-ready, are then sent off to be printed.

Indexer

The indexer usually reads the page proofs, selecting words and phrases representing essential concepts in the book, which are used to produce an index. An indexer, often a contractor, is a detail-oriented person who usually performs high-quality work that rarely requires correction. In writing more than 50 books, I've had fewer than five opportunities to view or review an index before publication. Publishers do not often permit an author to scrutinize an index because it can result in increased time and costs with little quality improvement. However, the proofreader or PE usually checks over the index before the book goes to press.

Manufacturing Staff

Manufacturing, which involves printing and binding the book, is often contracted to large printing firms and binderies, which are sometimes located offshore (because they are less expensive options). Typically, there is no interaction between the printer and the author, since the manuscript is in its final form when manufacturing begins.

In rare cases, a printer will do a small press run so that the AE and PE, and sometimes the author, can look at the finished and bound product. This practice is uncommon unless the book includes unusual features, such as fold-out pages. Once any review has been completed and changes made, the full printing run will be performed, and books are boxed up and made ready for the distributor.

Distribution Staff

The publisher contracts professional distributors to ship printed, boxed books to the publisher's warehouse and the warehouses of large retailers such as Barnes & Noble and Amazon.

Marketing Staff

Unless you are Stephen King or J.K. Rowling, it is unlikely that you will see billboards or big ads in airports promoting your latest book. Instead, good publishers will send you a generic book marketing kit that will contain helpful information and many ideas about how to promote your book. For the most part, you're responsible for promoting your book, but working with marketing people in the publishing company will help your sales. Chapter 6 explores marketing and promotion.

Merchandising Staff

Merchandising refers to how products are displayed in physical and online stores. You can impact online store sales by working with the AE and/or PE to determine how your book will be described and displayed by online retailers.

> **No One Works for Free**
>
> Earlier in this chapter, I discussed the typical royalty figures you're likely to earn from your book. Ten to fifteen percent may seem unreasonably small, but remember this: Publishers expend a significant amount of effort taking your idea from the rough draft (complete with errors) to books on a bookstore shelf. Your book is the product of considerable work by skilled professionals, and the result is quality work that is far superior to anything you could have done on your own. Trust me when I tell you that I still make 10–15 percent royalties after writing more than 50 books. I know that the other members of the book team turn my rough drafts into fine finished books that sell well. Without them, my books would be of far less quality. Writing a book is a team sport. Remember that.

Sales Staff

Some publishers employ salespeople who promote the newest books in their portfolios. For the most part, however, book sales are driven by demand buying through large retailers such as Amazon, Walmart, Barnes & Noble, and Books A Million. Higher education publishers have a direct salesforce that visits professors and department heads in universities to promote their latest textbooks.

> **NOTE:** As an author, your implicit responsibility is to understand the roles of everyone on the team and how you are expected to work with each of them. Having good relationships with everyone on the team is essential.

Your Book and Your Day Job

If you have a day job (and most writers do), it is vital that you keep your corporate job separate from your writing. After all, your employer is not paying you to moonlight. In addition, no aspect of your book writing can use any resource that belongs to your employer. To use an information security term, it is essential that you "air gap" your work life from your writing life.

Here are some examples to illustrate this concept:

- **Computer**   You must write your book using your own laptop or desktop computer. Do not use your corporate laptop or desktop for any aspect of your book at any time. There should be no trace or evidence of your writing on your corporate laptop or desktop computer, ever.

- **Internet resources**   You must use personal resources such as e-mail and file storage to support your writing. Your publisher should never, ever send an e-mail to you at your corporate e-mail address.

- **Time**   You must write your book after business hours and not at any time when your employer expects you to be on the job. You must successfully navigate the gray area between your work and personal lives. That said, I'll go on the record to say that I do have an occasional phone call with a co-author or someone in the publishing company from time to time, even when I'm at work. These are infrequent, however—maybe three or four times a year, even when I am writing more than one book in a single year.

- **Information**   You must never use information from your corporate job to support your writing project. If your technical book's topic includes techniques or technologies used by your employer, you must get your information elsewhere. I recommend you document your information sources in the unlikely event that your employer asks where you obtained the information used in your book.

- **Expertise of others**   Be very careful when asking co-workers questions about things you need to know for your book. If your inquiries are not related to your job, such a dialogue puts you on a slippery slope regarding the use of employer resources for a personally beneficial project. When you ask co-workers questions, you are using their work time and yours. In addition, they may be revealing intellectual property or trade secrets that could land you in serious trouble if they appear in your book, including criminal theft and disclosure of intellectual property.

It is vital that you maintain both the appearance and the fact of the complete separation between your work life and your writing life. You should in no circumstances engage in conduct that could be included in any of the examples cited.

> **Writing a Book for Your Employer**
>
> You may be one of the fortunate few who are writing a book as a part of their day job. In this case, you may be able to spend part of your workday on your book, and you'll probably have access to all of the information you need, including non-public information. One possible downside—although you will indeed be a published author, the royalties may belong to your employer.

Corporate Code of Conduct

Before you embark on your book project, become familiar with your work organization's intellectual property policies, moonlighting policy, and code of conduct. You need to be sure that your writing project does not infringe upon any of these policies, especially because you probably signed a contract that outlines these policies when you started your job.

To be sure of your standing regarding corporate policies, have a conversation about your writing project with an attorney in the corporate legal department or perhaps with the head of human resources. Their concerns will include the following:

- Whether you are revealing intellectual property or trade secrets
- Whether you are writing during work hours or using corporate resources
- Whether you are profiting from on-the-job experience or training that the company paid for

As I have done in the past, you might suggest that the corporate legal department review your book's TOC or even the entire manuscript. You'll benefit from a position of transparency instead of one of concealment. I would advise against requiring them to sign an NDA to view your manuscript. If, however, you do not trust your employer, you may be in a tricky position with little maneuvering room.

If you believe that your employer has not treated you fairly, you might consider consulting an attorney. However, I recommend that you proceed with caution here and limit your legal help to obtaining legal advice only. Barging into the corporate saloon with guns drawn will put your employer on the defensive and can be viewed as an adversarial move.

Intellectual Property and Publishing

One of my employers had an intellectual property and publishing policy requiring employees to obtain permission to write a book before doing so. I used this policy successfully and disclosed every book deal I was considering in advance. On one occasion, my employer's legal counsel advised that I not write a particular book because the subject matter appeared to promote a new technique that could compete with a service provided by my employer. I did not write that book because I wanted to avoid a legal skirmish with my employer, who had always been generous. Publishing one book to earn a few thousand dollars was not worth that risk.

Some employers' policies on intellectual property and publishing will state that the employer automatically owns all intellectual property created by its employees during the term of their employment, regardless of whether such intellectual property was created on the job using corporate resources or at home using personal resources. Since many publishers retain all rights to published works, you'll need to navigate this point carefully and tell your employer that you have no say in the matter and that the publisher owns the published work. Generally, an employer cannot legally forbid you from moonlighting, but they do not take kindly to employees profiting on the side from the company's intellectual property.

If you have a literary agent, they may be able to help with intellectual property concerns by providing you with talking points, negotiation tactics, or legal advice if your agent has access to legal counsel.

Corporate Bragging Rights

Depending upon your employer's line of business, and the topic of your book, your authoring a book could be viewed as a plus by your employer. In other words, your employer may recognize your technical leadership because your work is being published. Publishing a book is often viewed as an important professional achievement, giving you additional status in the organization. However, don't expect a salary increase, as your employer may realize that you are profiting from your writing.

Compartmentalize Your Writing Life

Depending upon your employer's temperament regarding your writing, generally speaking, you're best off if you completely separate your work life from your writing life. This could mean refraining from talking about your writing while you're at work, and even being silent and not announcing that your book has been published. If your employer is merely tolerating your writing, announcing your book's publication could be received as your "rubbing their nose in it." Authoring could sour your relationship with your employer, which I advise you avoid at all costs.

I have been most fortunate because my employers have celebrated with me as my books have been published. Being a modest individual,

I do not make a big deal about my books at work, but I'm not entirely silent about it either. In fact, at one point in my writing career, I was hired in part because of my writing experience. But writing books can be a two-edged sword. I've been hired, and fired, for writing.

4   THE WRITING PROCESS

After purchasing this book, if you have come straight to this chapter, please STOP! You are not ready. You are no more prepared than an engineer who wants to build a bridge that has not yet been designed. Seriously. Writing a book does not begin with writing. It starts with several layers of planning, which are covered in Chapters 1, 2, and 3.

When you have completed the planning described in these chapters, you are almost ready to begin writing. *Almost.* You need to do some final preparation steps before you start, or as soon as possible after you start. This chapter describes a methodology for storing your chapter files, keeping track of your progress, creating or acquiring illustrations, and protecting your content if your technology fails you.

Setting Up Your Tech

The business of writing requires that you have the right tools for the job. It helps if you have computing hardware, software, and appropriately licensed and reliable tools. Your system must perform in top condition when you need it. After you have signed a contract with a publisher to write your book, your computer and its software are now considered work tools, not merely a means for correspondence, online shopping, or entertainment.

Hardware

Your computer should be new enough to support the latest version of Windows, macOS, Linux, or ChromeOS. The newest version, or at least a recent version, will be supported by the manufacturer with security patches and other fixes, making your system stable and protecting it. Your system should have plenty of RAM (8GB is considered a minimum for most OSs) and hard drive storage, enough to hold multiple copies of chapter files, image files, research material, and multiple books if you keep on writing. I consider 250GB the lowest amount of hard drive storage you'll need.

If you use a laptop, think about using an external monitor. Often, you'll have multiple documents and one or more worksheets open at the same time. Having them all on display simultaneously is far better than moving between them, one at a time. Use the largest and highest resolution monitor (or multiple monitors) that you can reasonably afford. I wrote several books on a small Compaq laptop with no external display, which was quite tedious. Today, I use a large 4K monitor, which makes working on multiple files far easier.

Operating System

As I mentioned, your computer should be running a current or recent version of the OS—recent enough that the manufacturer still issues patches and fixes. Your OS should be a legit, licensed copy as well. You are in business now, and this is not just a hobby.

It's helpful if your system is dedicated to your writing, or at least optimized for it. Move your games to another computer so that they do not interfere with your writing or consume excessive resources. Organize your desktop and tools menus to make writing easy and convenient.

Configure your OS to notify you of software updates and patches. However, you may not want your OS to install them automatically because this may lead to reboots that occur when you're not ready.

You need to control the installation of updates to avoid losing any work.

The stability of your OS is essential. When you are writing, try to avoid having many other programs running on your system that consume resources and affect the system's stability. Ideally, your OS will run for days and weeks at a time, with only infrequent reboots, which will enable you to avoid having to reopen your chapter files, tracking worksheets, and reference documents.

Data Storage

Storage is critical on a system used for writing. The last thing you need is to be in the middle of writing a book on a machine that's nearly out of disk space, so you must constantly find other files to delete to make room for your manuscript, images, and research materials. If your system is in such a condition, consider upgrading the internal storage, moving other information to another storage system, or acquiring another system and dedicating it to your writing.

In addition to the main disk storage in your computer, you'll need one or more external hard drives or SSDs for backing up your book and research files. Hard drives and even SSDs can fail, and losing your work would be disastrous.

Many calamities can quickly destroy your system and even your backup data, including fire, flood, lightning, robbery, and theft. Any of these could completely wipe out all your hard work. For this reason, you should seriously consider cloud-based storage for backing up all your book-related data. Cloud-based storage is practically free, and I recommend that you use it to make remote backups of everything. If you already use cloud-based storage, create a folder to separate your writing from your other stored content. Ensure that your cloud storage is accessible only by you and that you implement the strongest security available, including multifactor authentication, so that no one else can break in and steal your files.

Writing Tools

You'll be writing your book using a word processor, most likely MS Word, but possibly Google Docs, LibreOffice, FrameMaker, or another program. It's imperative that you follow your publisher's guidance here; if they specify that you use Word, you must use Word. Although other tools such as Google Docs can create documents in a Word-like format, some differences can be difficult for the publisher to deal with. Although it's not free, MS Word is not so expensive to be worth the trouble of using a different tool and dealing with formatting differences and angst from editors. Your word processor is the core of your work toolset, so you need to use what is required—and use a legitimately licensed copy. If in doubt, talk to your AE or PE to understand your choices.

Business E-mail and Website

You'll send and receive a considerable amount of e-mail correspondence while pitching, writing, and promoting your book. This is business correspondence, and you need to take good care of it. Consider using a separate e-mail account for your writing, versus other personal e-mail account(s). And remember, by no means should you *ever* use your day-job e-mail for publishing!

Consider building a website for your writing business that includes information about you, your books, and the subject matter of your books. Numerous free and low-cost platforms are available that enable you to establish a legitimate and valuable web presence in a matter of a few hours. Also, consider buying a domain name that would point to your website; if you decide to change to a different website platform in the future, your domain name will continue to be valid.

Your book will probably include information that helps readers contact you, whether by e-mail or through your domain name. On my website, a person can type in their name, e-mail, and a message on a contact form, and the message is sent to me via e-mail. I do not reveal my e-mail address in my books or on my website because this invites too much spam.

Workspace

You need a quiet, comfortable space in which to write. Your workspace, typically a home office, should be away from activities that may interrupt your work. Writing often requires intense concentration and much time to think. At times, you'll have writer's block, when the words do not come freely, and you'll appreciate a space for deep, uninterrupted thought to get back on track. Writing in the dining room where family and noises abound will not help your productivity.

The ergonomics and lighting for your workspace are critical. I'm not an expert in either, but I appreciate when they're right and suffer when they're not. Your comfort and health depend on this.

You'll need space for more than your computer, keyboard, mouse or trackpad, and a cup of coffee. You'll also need sufficient desk space to accommodate having one or more other books open, especially if you'll be referring to content in those books. Get yourself a book weight, a handy thing for keeping a book open, such as the one shown in Figure 2. You'll wonder how you ever got along without it.

As you set up your home office, give serious consideration to electrical outlets. Make sure there are sufficient outlets nearby, and avoid overloading them. Consider purchasing a UPS (uninterruptible power supply) so that any power bumps or outages do not cause you to lose your work. I recommend you do this even if you are writing on a laptop computer; in an extended outage, you want to have time and available energy to copy your work to an external hard drive.

Figure 2. A book weight makes it easier to read book passages as you work (source: author).

Lab Space

Often, as you're writing, you may need to have other equipment running so that you can test procedures, take screenshots, and take photographs. Additional computers will require extra space and perhaps more lighting and electrical outlets. Don't overload electrical circuits, and make sure that powering up and down your lab gear doesn't result in surges that will affect your writing computer.

Suppose your book is about hardware or software that runs on a personal computer. In that case, I highly recommend you do your testing and experimenting on a computer that is separate from the computer you use to write your book. This way, problems encountered on one computer won't affect the other.

My System

I'm fortunate to have a nice setup for writing. Today, my hardware and software for writing books include the following:

- 2019 MacBook Pro 16 in. (16GB RAM and 1TB SSD) running macOS Big Sur, sitting atop an adjustable aluminum stand (this replaced my 2008 aluminum unibody MacBook, which, until this year, still ran and with which I wrote many books)

- External wired Apple full keyboard and Apple Magic Trackpad
- Apple Time Capsule for Time Machine backups
- Several external hard drives from Apricorn for Time Machine backups, which are stored in various places
- Acer 34 in. 4K monitor
- Asus portable 15 in. 1920×1080 USB monitor to use when traveling
- iPhone 11 Pro for taking photographs
- Two CyberPower UPS systems—a smaller one for our incoming Internet and a larger one for my laptop and Time Capsule
- A whole-house Siemens FS140 surge protector
- Linksys Velop full mesh Wi-Fi
- Office 365, including Word, Excel, PowerPoint, and OneNote apps installed
- Grammarly Editor Premium app
- Adobe Acrobat Reader
- Brave Browser with some security-related extensions
- NordVPN for protecting my communications
- Several security programs, including Cylance Smart Antivirus, Sophos, and Malwarebytes
- A cloud storage provider to which I back up my publishing files using the FreeFileSync incremental backup tool
- Website hosted on WordPress, with my domain name registered with a secure service in privacy mode that does not reveal any contact information

- E-mail and other Google services protected with Google Advanced Protection

Figure 3 shows my usual desk setup.

I wrote my first book, *Solaris Security*, using FrameMaker on my Sun SPARCstation 10 computer. I violated my principle of using a separate computer for writing because I could afford only one Sun workstation at first. Before I wrote my second book, *Sun Certified System Administrator for Solaris 8 Study Guide*, I purchased a used Sun Ultra 1. I used both computers to set up the various networking scenarios required for screenshots and explaining things correctly.

Figure 3. Author's writing tools (source: author).

I purchased a Compaq laptop in 2004 and wrote several books on it, using only the included tiny display, trackpad, and keyboard. My next laptop was a 2008 Unibody MacBook, which still runs today but is retired from daily work. I used two Chromebooks for writing *Chromebook For Dummies*, 2nd edition, in 2018.

Tax Benefits

Whether you are self-publishing or have a contract with a publisher, remember that you're running a writing business. Hence, certain tax benefits are available as a small business owner. These benefits include the ability to write off some of your expenses related to the purchase of hardware, software, subscriptions, and business use of a portion of your home. I also recommend you consider creating a business entity such as an LLC (Limited Liability Company) and that you have your publisher pay the LLC instead of paying you directly.

I use the services of a professional accountant and a lawyer, and I recommend you do the same.

Your Writing Schedule

Depending upon many factors, including the length of your book and the details it contains, count on taking dozens to a few hundred hours in total to write your first draft. Unless you are retired or earning passive income (such as Social Security or a pension), you probably have a day job and perhaps family and other obligations. Realistically, you may be able to put in one to three hours each day, or perhaps you can devote a good part of a weekend day each week to writing. This means that it will take several months to a year or more to write your book.

To succeed in your book project, you'll need to establish a set schedule, whatever that might be: early mornings, late evenings, Saturday mornings—whatever. And if you've signed on with a publisher, you've contracted to finish the book in a specified amount of time, and this will affect how much time you'll need to spend writing to meet your deadlines.

I recommend that you negotiate your writing schedule with your family members. You will need their support so that they will respect your boundaries (like trying to leave you alone during your writing time so that you can make steady, even if slow, progress). It's unwise to expect that your spouse or other family members will take on all of your family and household responsibilities—this also needs to be negotiated. Be reasonable, and hopefully, you can find an arrangement that works for you.

Early in my writing career, I wrote in the evenings a few days each week after putting the kids to bed. I would write until I was literally falling asleep at the computer, and my progress was slow. A colleague suggested that I instead write early each morning before other family members were awake; this was great advice, as my productivity and quality improved dramatically.

For years, I wrote early in the morning and half of a weekend day each week. After moving to the country, we had more household and property responsibilities, so I shifted my writing schedule again. Now I write only on weekday mornings and not at all on weekends.

Whatever schedule you establish, find the discipline to stick with it, but be willing to make adjustments so that you are not neglectful of your other obligations, particularly your family relationships.

Getting Organized

You'll accumulate many individual files as you write your book, likely more than 100 in all. As a professional writer, you're responsible for organizing them in a way that keeps you from getting confused or losing things.

In my early writing days, I suffered through the pain caused by disorganization, and I don't want you to suffer the same way. Getting things mixed up can waste much time and possibly frustrate the publisher as well if you're submitting the wrong files.

I use a time-proven hierarchy for storing files for each book project, and I'm pretty sure my system will work for you as well. The following outline describes what I use to keep everything organized.

- **Top folder**   Name includes the book title, with several subfolders.

- o **Legal**   Contracts and other legal matters for this book only.
- o **Research.**   Vendor files, whitepapers, and other references.
- o **Correspondence**   I store it here instead of leaving it buried in e-mail, with a **Copyright** subfolder for PDFs of important e-mails, such as permissions to use copyrighted material.
- o **Manuscript**   The book manuscript, plus several subfolders. (The number in front of each subdirectory name reflects chronological order.) Within each subfolder, I sometimes create an **Archive** subfolder for files no longer needed (better than deleting them, in case you need them later).
  - **0 – First Draft**   First draft files
  - **1 – Project Editor**   Revisions sent from the PE
  - **2 – Tech Editor**   Revisions from the TE
  - **3 – Copy Editor**   Revisions from the CE
  - **4 – Proof**   Page proofs
  - **Figures**   In books with many images, I create subfolders for each chapter.
- o **Reader Feedback**   Important correspondence and other info from readers.
- o **Errata**   Notes about errors I've found or others have found.
- o **Marketing**   Information related to promoting my book after publishing.
- o **Work Papers**   Other information.

On my computer, my top-level organization looks like this:

- **Pub**   A folder in My Documents.
  - o **Publisher Name**   Each publisher I have written for.
    - **Book Title**   Each book written for a specific publisher (the Top Folder in the preceding outline).

> **Scrivener**
>
> The Scrivener writer's app is fondly known as the "writer's shoebox" because it helps an author organize everything: manuscript, notes, research, figures, and creating your final manuscript in Word, PDF, Final Draft, or plain text. Its Corkboard planning tool helps an author stay organized. The Outliner is used to develop the structure of a book. Scrivener works on Windows, Mac, and iOS. I know a few people who use Scrivener and derive significant value from it. I don't use it myself, but don't take that as a lack of endorsement, as it is highly regarded in the writing world.

Formatting Document Files

Publishers often require that your book's content follow various formatting rules. Your publisher will provide information on how to format your content so they can work with it. Do your book team a favor and use the appropriate template and formatting as you write your book.

Many publishers will provide an author's guide that explains many aspects of manuscript creation and formatting. This publication may describe the required formatting for chapter files, or the publisher may include a sample chapter file that illustrates all the different types of styles used in the book. If your publisher does not offer this type of guidance, it's reasonable to request a sample chapter from another book (they'll clean it up for you) so that you have a tangible standard you can refer to as you write.

If you're an experienced writer and working for a new publisher, talk with your PE so that you can better understand the publisher's expectations for style, format, revisions, and so on. A few minutes of discussion can help save you, and the rest of the book team, time reworking a file if it's formatted incorrectly.

If your publishing arrangement asks you to submit the entire book draft at once, it's still wise to send the publisher a completed chapter early in the project. The AE and/or PE can look it over and confirm that the formatting and styles are correct, or they may give you helpful feedback so that you can format all your subsequent chapters correctly. Everyone is better off knowing these details and getting them right early in the process.

Using Template Files

Larger publishers require that authors attach the publisher's custom template to their manuscript documents. The template contains pre-formatted settings that are attached to your document, such as page margins, paragraph spacing, font sizes, heading styles, and other important formatting information. This is necessary to maintain a consistently formatted document throughout the editing and revision processes, and it helps the compositor work with the files later down the line. A consistently formatted document allows the CE to check the heading levels, text formatting, and other important elements. These template files are often MS Word .dot files.

If you are new to templates, it's essential that you become familiar with them. There is ample free learning material on using template files on the Internet. The publisher's PE or author guidelines may be of help as well, but do not expect the PE to teach you the fundamentals—after all, you are a professional author, and you're expected to know how to create a good manuscript.

> **Template Disaster**
>
> Years ago, I was writing a book for a major publisher. My book was the first to be published in a new size and layout format, and the publisher created a new template to attach to my book document that other authors would follow later on. The book was fun to write, and I thoroughly enjoyed working with the PE, who took the time to explain how to use the template—part of what made this project a great experience.
>
> One day, the PE called to tell me some bad news: The publisher had made a mistake on the page dimensions in the template file. The result was that my book was dozens of pages over the budgeted page count, and we had to remove 20 or 30 pages from the completed rough draft. We had little time (only a few days) to complete this work and stay on schedule.
>
> Fortunately, the PE was experienced, and we worked through the situation together. This issue occurred in the days before PC-based videoconferencing and screen sharing, so we worked on our respective draft manuscript chapters to decide what would stay and what would go for each section. Other changes were required to knit the new shortened manuscript together neatly with no loose ends (such as references to sections that had been removed). Overall, the book turned out quite well, and although it is more than 10 years old, it still sells today (though at low volumes).
>
> Incidentally, I took many of the deleted passages and created a humorous "outtakes" website for the book. When life hands you lemons, make lemonade!

Naming Book Files

Throughout the entire book writing and revision process, you're going to have dozens to hundreds of files to deal with. Determining a system for naming files, or using a system developed by the publisher, will help you and the publisher identify the contents of each file by its name. (Note that your filenames should not be used as your only method of writing recordkeeping. Hopefully, you'll use a detailed set of spreadsheets to track the progress of your project, carefully and file-by-file.)

Many publishers require that you follow specific naming guidelines for chapter files and other book-related files, and this will be specified in the materials you've hopefully received. Because publishers and project teams are working on several books simultaneously, the file naming convention should include information that uniquely identifies your book from all others, often the book's ISBN (International Standard Book Number), a number used by the publishing industry to identify each unique book. Using this method also helps in case a book file is misplaced. If the publisher doesn't require the use of a file naming convention, you'll need to develop a scheme of your own to help you stay organized.

Generally, your book will involve two types of files: chapter files and illustration files, which may include images of various kinds. Both types of filenames should uniquely identify the author, the book, and the particular chapter or chronological figure number. For example, if I am working on a book on network security, the name of my Chapter 1 file might be **Gregory NetSec Ch01.docx**.

Similarly, you'll need to name your image files consistently. You might be tempted to use a file naming convention such as **Gregory NetSec Fig 6-3.png** to represent Figure 3 in Chapter 6, but I've discovered a better idea. I suggest you decouple the image filenames from the figure numbers (this is explained in the next section, "Keeping Track of Your Work"). Use a naming convention similar to this: **Gregory NetSec Fig0001.png, Gregory NetSec Fig0002.png**, and so on. Then, in your workbook, described in the next section, you can associate the Fig0001.png and Fig0002.png files with their actual chapter locations in your book.

I suggest this image file naming scheme for one reason: Throughout your book project, you'll often be adding images, removing images, and moving images within and among chapters. In some projects, this may happen a lot, and it would get confusing to have to rename every image file each time this occurs. Chances are, you'll goof something up in your renaming, resulting in images appearing in the wrong places or even being/getting lost altogether. Trust me on this. I had to learn the hard way.

Keeping Track of Your Work

I used to pride myself on my ability to keep track of things and remember details. All of that changed when I wrote my first book. As is usual for a tech book, I submitted early chapters, some of which were in various tech review stages, while others were with the CE. I was still writing the drafts of later chapters. Files were coming in and going out almost every day. Further, I took photographs and created illustrations, and these files were also bounding about in e-mail and on my computer.

Making matters worse, I had not yet concocted an organizational scheme with directories and subdirectories to keep all these files neat and orderly. Though I am detail-oriented, I was entirely new at this and did not know how to organize this dizzying array of details. My project was a hot mess.

Believing I had learned these lessons, I was marginally better while writing my second and third books. Still, though, it wasn't easy to know the precise status of each book file.

My failure to track each file's status thoroughly was one of my most painful writing experiences. I'm mentioning this hoping that you can learn from my early mistakes and choose to adopt a method of recordkeeping that can help keep you sane and keep your book project on track.

Create a Writing Project Tracker

As I write this, my 51st book manuscript, I have developed a time-proven project tracker that tracks every chapter file, every illustration (including rights management), and more. Each book has somewhat different requirements, but the basics are always the same. I'll explain.

I use Microsoft Excel, but you can use any spreadsheet program for this. There are few formulas, only grids of cells to keep track of everything.

First Tab: Chapter Status

I spend a lot of time working in the Chapter Status tab, where I keep track of each chapter file, from creation through final proofreading, plus all the back and forth in between. The rows of this tab represent the chapter files themselves. I use these column names:

- Chapter number
- Chapter name
- Page count target
- Due date
- Draft
    - Date writing started
    - Date writing completed
    - Page count [1]
- Project editor review
    - Date received from the project editor
    - Date sent back to the project editor
- Tech editor review
    - Date received from the project editor
    - Date sent back to the project editor
- Copy editor review
    - Date received from the project editor
    - Date sent back to the project editor

---

[1] Often, I will include a formula to total the number of pages of the book.

- Page proofing
  - Date received from the project editor
  - Date sent back to the project editor
  - Final page count

I also use colors that serve as status flags that help me focus on tasks. Here are some examples:

- When I start writing a chapter draft, I type in the date I started it and highlight the cell in yellow to draw attention to it as an active part of the project. When I complete the chapter, I send it to the publisher, fill in the date completed, and change the start and end date cells from yellow to green, signifying the completion of this phase for the chapter.

- When I receive a chapter from the PE for any subsequent project phases (such as tech editing and copy editing), I save the file to the appropriate subdirectory, add the date received on the worksheet, and highlight the date received cell in yellow. This color highlighting signifies that I have a chapter file in some stage of review that requires my attention. When I complete the processing of the chapter file, I send it to the publisher, add the date, and highlight the cell in green.

When I start a new book, I build the complete matrix, with its rows of chapter numbers, names, page count targets, due dates, and so on, plus the column headings for all the editing stages. Before I start writing, the grid cells are all blank (except for page count target and due date). Then, as the project progresses, the dates begin to fill in, and I can see steady progress in the project. Figure 4 shows this grid for a book I am working on now, *CIPM Certified Information Privacy Manager All-in-One Exam Guide*. I have completed all the chapter drafts in this example, and the TE has likewise completed his review. Copy editing is partially done, and no proofreading has been completed.

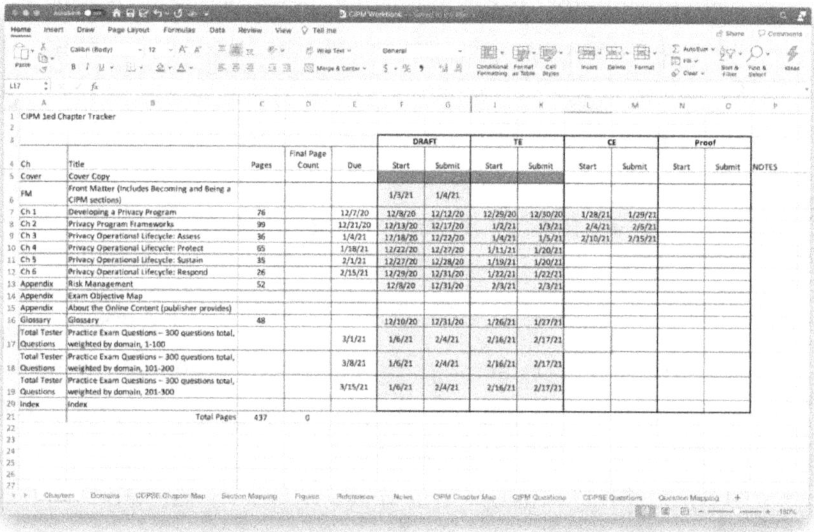

CIPM 3ed Chapter Tracker

Ch	Title	Pages	Final Page Count	Due	DRAFT Start	DRAFT Submit	TE Start	TE Submit	CE Start	CE Submit	Proof Start	Proof Submit	NOTES
Cover	Cover Copy												
FM	Front Matter (Includes Becoming and Being a CIPM sections)				1/3/21	1/4/21							
Ch 1	Developing a Privacy Program	76		12/7/20	12/8/20	12/12/20	12/29/20	12/30/20	1/28/21	1/29/21			
Ch 2	Privacy Program Frameworks	99		12/21/20	12/13/20	12/17/20	1/2/21	1/3/21	2/4/21	2/5/21			
Ch 3	Privacy Operational Lifecycle: Assess	36		1/4/21	12/18/20	12/22/20	1/4/21	1/5/21	2/10/21	2/15/21			
Ch 4	Privacy Operational Lifecycle: Protect	65		1/18/21	12/22/20	12/27/20	1/11/21	1/20/21					
Ch 5	Privacy Operational Lifecycle: Sustain	35		2/1/21	12/27/20	12/28/20	1/19/21	1/20/21					
Ch 6	Privacy Operational Lifecycle: Respond	26		2/15/21	12/29/20	12/31/20	1/22/21	1/22/21					
Appendix	Risk Management	52			12/8/20	12/31/20	2/3/21	2/3/21					
Appendix	Exam Objective Map												
Appendix	About the Online Content (publisher provides)												
Glossary	Glossary	48			12/10/20	12/31/20	1/26/21	1/27/21					
Total Tester Questions	Practice Exam Questions – 300 questions total, weighted by domain, 1-100			3/1/21	1/6/21	2/4/21	2/16/21	2/17/21					
Total Tester Questions	Practice Exam Questions – 300 questions total, weighted by domain, 101-200			3/8/21	1/6/21	2/4/21	2/16/21	2/17/21					
Total Tester Questions	Practice Exam Questions – 300 questions total, weighted by domain, 201-300			3/15/21	1/6/21	2/4/21	2/16/21	2/17/21					
Index	Index												
	Total Pages	437	0										

Figure 4. Sample chapter tracking worksheet (source: author).

Second Tab: Figure Status

The Figure Status tab of the workbook tracks all the book's numbered figures and illustrations. A full-length tech book can include dozens of images; this worksheet helps keep track of each one.

In my worksheet, each row is a different figure, and the columns are named as follows:

- **Filename.** I use a serialized scheme including the book title, such as CISSP FD Img0001.png.
- **Chapter number.** Each chapter gets its own column.
- **Figure number.** Each numbered figure gets its own column.
- **Status.** Indicates whether I have sketched the line art, taken the photo, or whatever. This is part of my figure planning. I add something like "Not Started" to remind me that I still need to acquire the image.
- **Submitted.** Date art is submitted to the publisher.
- **Caption.** Text for the actual caption used in the book.

- **Caption attribution.** The attribution text that appears for images obtained from external sources. Example: "Image courtesy of Cisco Systems."
- **Source.** The source of the image, generally the organization's or person's name.
- **Copyright model.** Examples include Open Source, Creative Commons, or other copyright and attributions models.
- **URL.** Location of an image obtained from a website.
- **Contact.** A contact at the organization (generally an e-mail address) with whom I will be corresponding to obtain written permission to use the image.
- **Permission Status.** This may be "Not requested," "Requested," "Pending," "Granted," "Denied," or freeform text that indicates the current permission status.
- **Notes.** Sometimes, there's more to track.

Depending on the details, I often include additional columns to help track the image catalog.

Third Tab: Rights Status

If I am using numerous borrowed illustrations, quotes, excerpts, and similar materials, I create a separate Rights Status tab to keep more detailed records than I include in the Figure Status tab. I organize the spreadsheet's columns like this:

- **Item name.** A simple name for content that I want to include in my book. Examples include "Intel Gantt Chart" for a Gantt chart appearing in an Intel Corporation publication, or "Phillip Rogers Quote" for an extended quotation from a work created by a person named Phillip Rogers.
- **Filename.** An illustration filename or a chapter filename (for an excerpt). I recommend against referencing items by figure number, since renumbering figures could cause confusion when tracking rights.

- **Source.** Where the original material appears, such as in a book, on a website (including a URL), or in another publication.
- **Contact.** One or more columns signifying the name and contact information for the person, group, or institution that owns the rights to the material.
- **Status.** The status of a request to use the work. Examples: "Not Started," "Requested," "Granted," or "Denied."
- **Copyright Model.** The type of copyright asserted for the work, if known.
- **Attribution.** How the work will be attributed in the book. Some copyright owners require specific wording.

NOTE: Save your correspondence with each copyright owner. If you use webmail, create PDFs of the e-mails that grant permission to use the work. Your publisher may require you to send copies of the e-mails (or other correspondence) for their records. If a copyright infringement issue occurs after your book is published, the publisher will likely be contacted, and they'll need ready access to these consents.

Fourth Tab: References

As you do research for your book, you may spend considerable time reading websites from vendors, researchers, customers, and others. As you run across websites, books, or other sources that you will use now or may access later, keep a record of them here. You may encounter a dizzying array of information sources—more than you can remember, if you're like most people. You don't want to rely solely on your browser history or your growing list of bookmarks.

You could also consider using the Mendeley Reference Manager tool if you prefer to maintain your references information online.

Fifth Tab: Notes

As your project progresses, an array of notes, facts, and other matters will come to mind. Create a Notes tab to keep track of these odds and ends. Often, these are "notes to self" reminders, and you might also include a Status column to indicate when you have completed these tasks. (You could then delete the line with the note when you complete the task, but I prefer to keep these around because they could be helpful later.)

For example, while writing an early chapter, suppose that you research some material relevant to what you're currently working on. You come across other information that you know you'll need to access for a later chapter. You can use the Notes tab to add a reminder to return to that reference later when you need it. Or suppose the TE is working on earlier chapters while you're writing later chapters. The TE comments on something from an earlier chapter that will also apply to later chapters. Use the Notes tab to capture this information so you won't forget.

Other Tabs

The nature of your book's subject matter may require that you keep track of facts, standards, protocols, techniques, or other items that aren't listed elsewhere, such as in the TOC. For instance, when working on a certification study book, I use workbook tabs to track practice questions, domain coverage, and other reference materials from the certification organization.

Including Graphical Elements

Tech books typically include three types of graphic images: line art, screenshots, and photographs. Your publishing contract may stipulate a maximum number of one or more of these. For instance, the contract may state that the publisher will render 20 rough line art sketches into camera-ready art. If you submit 15 images, you're okay, and if you submit 22, you're probably also fine. But if you turn in 40 images, you and the publisher will have a conversation to determine which images are necessary and which will be omitted.

Line Art

When I create line art, I sketch a figure on a notebook sheet, caption it, scan or photograph it, and send a JPG or PNG to the publisher. Figure 5 shows an example figure from my book, *CISSP For Dummies*, 3rd edition (co-authored with Larry Miller). Notice that I include the filename, chapter number, and figure number within the sketch. This way, the file documents itself. As you'll read in the section "Figure File Identification" later in this chapter, I now use a different system for naming figure files.

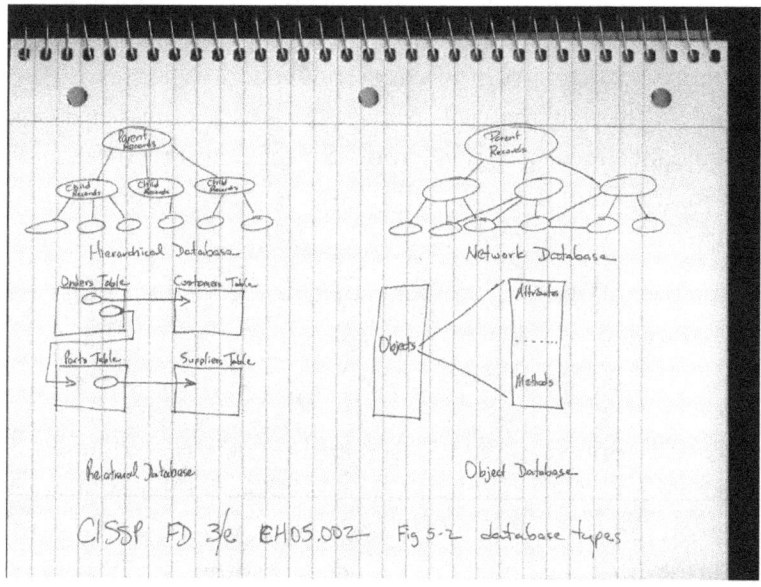

Figure 5. Sample line art provided to the publisher (source: author).

Each publisher and each project is different. At the start of the project, you need to understand what the publisher expects of you (and vice versa) regarding images. Most publishers have been okay with my hand-drawn sketches, and their artists can use my rendering to create camera-ready line art for use in the book. However, other publishers may expect the author to produce camera-ready art. In this case, they'll spell out their requirements, and you'll need to understand details regarding file formats, resolution, and other settings. They may require source files from Illustrator, Photoshop, PowerPoint, or other formats, or they may be fine receiving simple JPG or PNG files. Make sure your project schedule accommodates the time required to render these images.

Screenshots

Many tech books include screenshots of computers or devices to guide the reader visually through a procedure. You may obtain screenshots from vendors or create them yourself. In your figure attribution recordkeeping, you'll keep track of the source in each case.

Publishers generally provide authors with detailed guidance on capturing screenshots. During the compositing process, the compositor may be doing some image conversion to massage each screenshot into a format that will print nicely in the finished book. Publishers' guidance may specify the tools for making screen captures, and resolution and color settings. Often, this is the most prescriptive guidance imparted to authors.

If you anticipate taking large numbers of screenshots, a professional tool like Snagit may be invaluable.

Formatting

If your book will contain numerous screenshots, it's probably worth discussing with your PE to ensure that you understand the publisher's formatting requirements. Your PE may ask you to submit some samples to ensure that the images you send are appropriate. You don't want to be told later in the project that you need to reshoot dozens of images.

Colors

In tech books, images usually appear in black and white or grayscale. When you're producing screenshots, you should convert them yourself (even if the publisher requires color originals) to see whether the shades of color are rendered in a way that the reader can perceive; sometimes, different colors look the same when rendered in black and white. You'll need to follow the publisher's guidance regarding the background of screen captures (some require a white background to eliminate potential trouble with odd colors appearing in rounded window corners).

You may need to take more than one screenshot if your screenshot tool has resolution or color settings, or if you want to view different screenshot samples after changing color or appearance settings in the software you're shooting. This may be necessary to ensure that your screenshot can be accurately and effectively rendered in the book.

Simplicity Is Essential

When composing screenshots, particularly when making whole-screen images, you should make your desktop environment as clean as possible. The "noise level" should be as close to zero as possible to protect your privacy and reduce clutter and distraction. Ideally, your screenshots will show only the parts of programs (or websites or other featured content) relevant to the subject being discussed in the book.

I suggest you follow these guidelines:

- If you are shooting browser windows,
    - Use a simple default theme that is easy to read.
    - Hide your bookmarks bar, except for any bookmarks relevant to what you're discussing in the book—the world doesn't need to see your personal details.
    - Hide your browser extensions, unless they are relevant.
    - Show only browser tabs that are directly related to the accompanying text.
- Your computer desktop should be as clean as possible so that the image shows no files or folders except those relevant to the topic. You can use a simple OS-provided wallpaper if necessary. No other application windows should be open unless they are relevant.
- Menus, status bars, system tray, dock, and other onscreen elements should be as clean as possible; hide personal details.

Although you may be writing and taking screenshots on the same computer, your screenshots should appear to have been taken on a clean "lab" computer that you use only for your book.

Photographing the Screen

At times, the OS featured in your book is in a primitive state, and it's not possible to capture a screenshot. You may have to resort to taking a photograph of the screen, but note that this practice is almost always disastrous because your photo will contain an unavoidable and distracting moiré pattern. Figure 6 illustrates this problem in an image from *Chromebook For Dummies*, 2nd edition.

Figure 6. Moiré patterns are unavoidable when photographing a screen (source: Chromebook For Dummies, 2nd edition; John Wiley & Sons, publisher).

Photographs

Photographs are a staple in many tech books. Images of components and devices are often helpful for readers—after all, a picture paints a thousand words, right? Your photographs complete the story and give the reader added confidence as they learn new tech.

Smartphone cameras are generally adequate for these photographs. Still, occasionally a digital SLR camera is called for in trickier situations when you need more control for focus, exposure, or depth of field.

As with screenshots, your photographs will likely be rendered in grayscale in the finished book. If the publisher wants color originals, by all means, give them the color originals. If not, you should convert them yourself to see how they render and to confirm that the image shows the subject clearly and with sufficient contrast and definition. Figure 7 shows a photo I took for *Chromebook For Dummies*.

Figure 7. A photograph used in a tech book (source: Chromebook For Dummies, *2nd edition; John Wiley & Sons, publisher).*

Often, you'll be cropping photographs to eliminate any unnecessary distractions, but don't crop your images too tightly. You may submit original images along with cropped images to offer the compositor some choices regarding what to use in the final layout.

As with other content in your book, you need to keep track of all your photos and those you obtain from other sources. If you need to reshoot photos later, you can add the appropriate columns in the Figure Status tab in your workbook. Alternatively, you can create a new tab in your workbook to record facts about each photo you shot so that you don't have to remember all the details.

Manuscript Placeholders

As I'm writing a draft chapter, if I determine that a figure of some type is needed, I need to do two things: First, the text of the chapter itself must refer the reader to the appropriate image. For instance, I might write, "Figure X illustrates an example of a virtual private network connection." After that paragraph, I'll insert some text that reads, "Insert <*filename*> here," which is an instruction to the compositor, followed by a caption: "Figure X: A VPN connection." In both cases, I highlight the "Figure X" so that it stands out. Each publisher marks inserted images in a unique way; some may require you to enter specific text in a particular format or style to alert the compositor.

I use "Figure X" instead of an actual figure number as I write the draft. Until the draft is complete, I don't know whether I will decide to insert other images in the chapter or change the order of paragraphs or sections, thus changing the figure numbers. Renumbering figures is a chore, and I'd prefer to number figures once, when I am confident of their completeness and sequence.

Note that when you examine your book after layout in page proofs, the compositor will insert the actual figures precisely at, before, or after your placeholder. It is the compositor's job to figure out (pun intended) where on a finished page an illustration should appear. They'll place it as close to your reference as possible so that the reader can easily and logically reference it.

NOTE: Some publishers refer to figures and/or illustrations, and I do the same in this book. Figures are usually numbered and captioned images identified in the text preceding the image. Illustrations may or may not have captions, and they may or may not be numbered.

Figure File Identification

In my early books, I named my draft figure files using the chapter number and chapter-specific figure numbers. For example, the file for Chapter 5, Figure 3 in *CISSP For Dummies* would be **CISSP FD Ch5 Fig 3.png**. That was fine until I was confronted with the need to remove, move, or reorder a figure or two. This resulted in a confusing mess.

It's wise to disconnect figure filenames from figure numbers and let your recordkeeping serve as a translator between the two. If you must insert, move, or delete figures later, it's no big deal, and no figure file renaming is necessary. Just update the Figure Status tab on your worksheet.

> **NOTE:** You will be expected to create images when you write the chapter drafts and then submit them with each respective chapter file. You won't see them again until page proofs, when the figures and illustrations have been inserted into the chapter files. You essentially get one bite of the apple when it comes to double-checking your images. You need to check carefully that the compositor rendered and processed them correctly and inserted them into the correct places in the final chapters. Luckily, you'll have some help with this from a proofreader, who may catch anything you miss.

Updating Your TOC

As discussed in Chapters 1 and 2, your completed TOC will include one or two levels of detail. I didn't emphasize earlier that you're expected to stick to that original TOC as you develop and write your manuscript. Creating a detailed TOC before the book project begins helps a publisher know what content to expect; asking an author to stick to that TOC helps the publisher avoid changes that can increase costs and cause delays. Nevertheless, you may find that you need to rearrange chapter sections, or add or remove sections, as you get deeper into your subject matter.

Because you committed to a TOC at the start of your project, it's best to contact your AE and/or PE to explain the situation and describe any proposed changes. If the TE is involved at this point, they may weigh in as well. Even though you are the book's author and the SME on the topic covered by your book, you still need to share your thinking with your PE and/or AE, and you need to ask if it's okay to change the book's structure, especially if it's late in the game.

If the proposed change impacts the book's page count, you must talk to the PE about this. The publisher will have established a page count budget that you cannot exceed. If your TOC change is early enough in the book project timeline, you may be able to shorten or lengthen other chapters and sections to make up for your proposed change. However, if your TOC change occurs late in the project, you may need to rework content already drafted and submitted. Any revisions will add time to the project—another complication the publisher needs to deal with. If your proposed change requires that the PE, TE, CE, or others down the line devote additional time to the book, especially if it requires re-editing, the publisher will need to address this and determine the potential impact (time and/or money) on this and other projects before you can go ahead and make the changes.

The later you are in your project, the less leeway and tolerance the publisher will have to accommodate any significant changes. Rework is expensive and delays your book—and potentially other books as well.

Co-authoring

As you know by now, writing a book as a sole author is a complicated undertaking. If you're writing a book with a co-author, you might think that your work would be easier, but co-authoring adds to the complication and presents other challenges.

Division of labor is challenge number one. You and your co-author(s) need to come to a solid agreement on what work each of you will perform. This arrangement should be in writing, and the AE and PE should be informed of who is writing what.

The challenges presented by a multi-author book include the following:

- **Chapter references** Often, passages in one section or chapter of a book will refer the reader to other sections or chapters. These references may be tricky if one author isn't sure that the co-author's chapter includes the referenced information.

- **Voice**   Co-authors should attempt to use a consistent voice, tense, tone, and style, as though a single author wrote the book.

Co-author Workflow

I have co-authored with four different writers on several projects. We divided the work so that we each worked on different chapters. Before submitting our first drafts to the publisher, each of us would send our first drafts to the other so that we had the opportunity to check for consistency issues. This approach added time to the overall project, however. In this case, the PE and the rest of the publishing team were aware of the modified workflow and extra time required, so they adjusted the schedule to accommodate our reviews.

Co-authoring requires more complicated recordkeeping. Your tracking worksheets will be more detailed because they need to reflect the additional steps of passing draft chapters back and forth between authors before sending them to the publisher. Further, you need to determine the scheme for technical editing and copy editing chapter files: Are they to be returned to the author who wrote them or to the co-author? My preference is that the creator of a chapter manages all copy editing of that chapter.

Tech editing is another matter. All co-authors should review the TE's comments and suggested changes, because they may apply to other parts of the book. For instance, if a TE comments on a co-author's notation on a specific technology in one chapter, this comment may apply to all subsequent mentions throughout the book.

Workload Issues

Co-authors need to formally document the division of labor at the start of the project. The publisher's contract probably won't include individual chapter assignments and other tasks; it will only mention the percentage of each author's royalties. For instance, one co-author may have a 60 percent share of royalties while the other has a 40 percent share. It's up to the co-authors (with the PE's involvement, perhaps) to deal with the details.

Life has a way of imposing unexpected circumstances upon us, resulting in delays and quality issues. Co-authors, together with the PE, need to keep lines of communication open so that delays and other issues are detected and dealt with early on.

Some measure of grace is appropriate. For instance, a co-author can offer to help another co-author finish a chapter or process the co-author's copy editing feedback if required. Publishers don't want to hear about petty workload issues because it is disruptive to the overall process. However, significant matters of productivity need to be addressed, and in extreme cases, this could result in contract addendums and reallocation of royalties.

Writer's Block

You may sit down to write, but you simply can't find the words. I've experienced writer's block more times than I can count. Unfortunately, there is no vaccine and certainly no herd immunity to relieve this affliction.

When you're stuck and don't know how to begin, one or more of the following ideas might help. Have all these remedies at your disposal, because you may need to use more than one to get back on track:

- Move on from what you're trying to write and try to begin writing in a different section or chapter.
- Switch to dictation if you're typing, or switch to typing if you're dictating.
- Take a break. Take a walk outside and look around.
- Start typing, focusing on a single word at a time. Don't think about the big picture.

Ironically, I put off writing this section until everything else in this chapter was completed. It was difficult for me to figure out how to put this into words!

A representation of writer's block by Leonid Pasternak (1862–1945) (source: image in the public domain).

Content Protection

The longer you write, the more likely you will encounter some issue that results in your losing parts of your written content—or even everything on your computer. Over the years, I've had to do no less than three "bare metal restore" operations (reinstalling the OS from backup or over the network from Apple), because of either a hard drive failure or some software bug that corrupted the entire hard drive.

(Windows computers are no more secure or reliable, by the way; I just happen to be a Mac—and iPhone and iPad—user.)

You can lose data, including manuscripts, illustrations, research, records, and more, in many ways:

- Malware attack
- Ransomware attack
- Phishing
- Hard drive crash
- File system corruption
- Software bug
- Accidental change
- Accidental deletion
- Lost password (if you are using Office 365 or Google Docs)
- Fire, flood, or other disaster
- Theft

Regardless of the event(s) that disrupts your writing project and requires you to re-create content, you are solely responsible for ensuring that any such events do not result in project delays. Remember that your book is not the only one in the publisher's pipeline; a delay in your project will affect all the publisher's other projects.

Back Up Your Content

Rather than waiting for a disaster to catch you off guard, you should develop a scheme for backing up all your project data so that you can quickly and easily restore it with minimum disruption. I back up data to a couple of local external hard drives that I keep in safe places. I also back up my project data to a secure, reputable cloud storage provider once or more each day. In addition, I back up the rest of my computer, including the OS, the software I use to write and manage my book projects, and other records, both locally and to two different cloud-based storage services.

Sooner or later, you're going to have to recover one or more files from backup. I recommend that you learn how to do this before you have a disruptive event to practice and become proficient at recovering data. An emergency is not the time to learn how.

Security

Once you become an author, you're no longer an amateur, but a writing professional. Your computer and the software you use are your work tools, and you need to up your security game to protect your livelihood. Several measures are required, including antimalware, spam/phishing protection, firewall protection, patching, and more. You must become more aware of the safety and security of your hardware and software.

Antimalware

Purchase business-grade antimalware (aka antivirus software). The free stuff is insufficient for a professional. Because you must rely on your work tools for your livelihood, the pro versions of antimalware are appropriate.

These are the best commercial antimalware programs for Windows:

- Norton 360
- Cylance Smart Antivirus
- McAfee Total Protection
- Trend Micro Maximum Security
- ESET NOD32 Antivirus

Here are the best commercial antimalware programs for Mac:

- Sophos Home Premium
- Cylance Smart Antivirus
- Avast Premium Security

- Bitdefender Antivirus for Mac
- Norton Security Deluxe

And these are the best antimalware programs for Chromebook:
- Bitdefender Mobile Security
- Malwarebytes Premium
- Norton Mobile Security
- Kaspersky Internet Security

NOTE: In the cybersecurity business, an individual vendor's fortunes may rise and fall, resulting in programs that were once highly recommended becoming those to avoid. Unless you are a cybersecurity expert, I recommend consulting with an expert to ensure that you have the best available protection.

Whether you use a Mac, a Windows PC, or a Chromebook, you need to be aware of the effectiveness of your antimalware software. In general, check periodically to ensure that it is successfully updating itself (at least once daily) and that it continues to protect your computer.

Many modern antimalware programs include a firewall program (or an easier way of managing the firewall that came with your computer's OS), browser protection, and other features. Be sure to use them all; threats can come from all sides.

Spam and Phishing Protection

Spam and phishing are serious problems today. Make sure that your e-mail service includes effective spam and phishing filtering that results in near-zero instances of spam arriving in your inbox. For spam that occasionally gets through, I suggest you immediately delete it without reading it. Some threats are carried within HTML content and can take over your computer. Talk about a bad day!

Firewall

If you use a laptop or notebook computer and occasionally (or frequently) use your computer online in various public places, it's crucial that you turn on your computer's firewall. Today, laptop firewalls are fairly easy to manage; many have a simple interface that lets you choose your protection strength. Select the strongest protection that still enables you to get your work done.

Disk Encryption

Modern OSs, including Windows and macOS, include built-in encryption for your computer's hard drive. Primarily, this protects the privacy of your data should your laptop be stolen. A criminal who steals your computer will not be able to read any of your data if the drive encryption is enabled.

Disk encryption comes into play only if you also activate an automatic screen lock. If you never lock your screen and someone steals your laptop, they're going to be able to get to all your data just by using File Explorer to look around. Set your automatic screen lock to a value that's not more than 15 minutes, and remember to lock your screen when you're away from your computer for more than a few minutes.

Up-to-Date OS and Software

Whether you use Windows and MS Office, a Mac, a Chromebook, or Google Docs, you must be diligent in keeping all your local software up-to-date and patched, including ancillary software such as Java and your browser(s). I recommend configuring the OS, MS Office tools, browsers, Java, and other software to download and automatically install all updates and patches.

Keeping software up-to-date is essential computer hygiene, akin to washing your hands often. Many of today's attacks are successful because people (and companies) do not keep their software updated and patched; this enables attackers to compromise target systems successfully to achieve whatever nefarious ends they have in mind.

Your browser is your window to the world. May I humbly suggest that you use one of these browsers, and be sure to keep them up-to-date:

- Firefox
- Brave (performs like Chrome and even supports Chrome browser extensions)
- Safari

Do be careful with browser extensions. Remove all that you do not need or actively use. Numerous malicious browser extensions can spy on you and cause other problems.

Secure Home Network

The security of your home (or office) network is an integral part of your overall computer security plan. Primarily, this means you'll play an active role in the configuration and security of your home router and/or Wi-Fi access point. Good practices include the following:

- Using nondefault administrative user ID and password
- Permitting administrative login only from inside your network
- Keeping the router/access point firmware up-to-date
- Turning on the firewall and using the highest setting
- Using the strongest possible security for your Wi-Fi network and changing the SSID from the factory default to some other value
- Having guest Wi-Fi and giving guests only the guest Wi-Fi access codes

If your Wi-Fi access point is more than five years old, consider getting a newer one. Consumer-grade routers and access points are notorious for not having current patches available. Attackers can easily break into older routers and access points. Don't let this include yours.

Virtual Private Network Software

If you spend even a little bit of time at locations where you're connecting to the Internet through others' Wi-Fi networks, I strongly suggest you obtain VPN software, not only for your laptop but for your smartphone as well. VPN software wraps all your laptop's network traffic in an encrypted envelope that makes it impossible for an adversary to eavesdrop on you or your communications, and it makes it more difficult for them to attack your computer directly.

Avoid free VPN! Free VPN is no bargain! If it's free, the makers are probably eavesdropping on your traffic on their VPN servers, or they are inserting advertising into your browsing. VPN costs money to operate, so to have a legitimate VPN, you will be paying a subscription fee. These are the best VPN services available today:

- Nord VPN (my personal favorite; it protects all our devices)
- ExpressVPN
- ProtonVPN
- SurfShark

Be sure to configure your VPN so that it's always on—at least when you're away from your home network and any other trusted networks.

NOTE: I have found that a limited number of apps or websites do not function while I'm using a VPN (primarily one of my online banking apps). You may need to take down your VPN from time to time. I sincerely hope that you will still use it most of the time.

Remote Locate and Kill

All Macs, iPhones, and iPads come with a "Find My" function that enables you to locate the physical position of all your devices in real-time and remotely erase a device if it is known to be lost or stolen. I suggest you take advantage of this feature.

Windows 10 has a similar feature that you can use to track your laptop's location if it is lost or stolen and remotely wipe its data. You must set up this capability with Apple products before your device is lost or stolen.

Password Security

Your data's security and privacy depend upon the security of the Internet services you use. Your best defense involves strong, unique passwords. The best way to achieve this is with a password vault. A password vault does two things: it provides highly secure storage for all your login credentials, and it generates strong, random passwords for new sites you sign up for (and for sites requiring you to change your password).

Here are the best password vault programs for Windows:
- Password Safe
- KeePass

Here are the best password vault programs for Macs:
- MacPass
- pwSafe

I've also seen good reviews of DashLane and LastPass, which work on PCs and Macs.

I strongly urge you NOT to use your browser for storing passwords. If a flaw was to be discovered in the protection of browser-stored passwords, a malicious website might be able to steal them all from you.

Insurance

As a professional writer, you may spend more money than the average consumer on computers, accessories such as monitors and storage devices, and software. The total value of these work tools may well exceed the coverage limits of your renter's or homeowner's insurance policy. You should ensure that, if you suffer from fire, flood, theft, or anything else that results in the loss of all your writing tools, your insurance will cover your losses.

While on the topic of insurance, you should also check to determine whether your personal liability insurance includes protection if you are sued by a publisher or another party concerning your writing. I suggest you consult with legal counsel, who can advise you on your liability, obtaining insurance, and establishing a corporation for your writing business.

5   THE REVISION PROCESS

Writing the first draft of your tech book is the first of many steps. As the author, you will participate in several stages of revisions, each undertaken by a different person and for a different reason. Your awareness of these steps will help you work smoothly and effectively throughout the publishing process, resulting in the best possible final product.

After turning in your last draft chapter, you still have work to do. Indeed, you are not even half done with your effort to turn your book from an idea into a completed manuscript.

The Front Matter

If a reader opens your book and reads from the beginning, the front matter is the first content they read. Depending on your publisher's style, the front matter will contain the following parts (not necessarily in this order):

- **Title page**   This includes your book's title, your name (and any co-author names), and the name of the publisher. Your publisher will provide this page for you. It may be preceded by a half-title page if your book title consists of a main title and a subtitle (as this book does).

- **Copyright page** The primary copyright statement, the ISBN, and other information about the publisher, such as address and contact information, are included on this page. Some publishers include a separate page with the names of those who have worked on the book (the book team), from the editors to the compositors.
- **Dedication** This short statement describes to whom you dedicate your book.
- **About the author** You'll provide the publisher with a short biography, including a brief description of your professional career, other books or literary projects you have completed, and other professional activities. You can also include information such as your outside interests, your family, and where in the world you call your home. Some publishers will also include similar information about the book's tech editor.
- **Table of contents** Unless you are self-publishing, the publisher will create the final version of the TOC.
- **List of tables and/or illustrations** This optional element includes a chronological list of all the tables and illustrations in the book, along with attributions.
- **Foreword** This is an introduction to your book, usually written by another expert in your field—often someone who is well known in the industry. In a technical book, a foreword is sometimes a formal, written endorsement for the book.
- **Acknowledgments** Usually written by the author, this section provides an opportunity to thank the people who have helped create the book, or those who have helped you professionally or personally in other ways.
- **Preface and/or introduction** Written by the author, this narrative is several pages in length and serves as an introduction to the entire book. You may provide historical context, explain why you wrote the book, or give some other background information or context.

Although this content appears at the front of your book, I urge you to write it last. Rather than the front matter being a summary of the book you *will write*, it should summarize the book you *have written*.

When possible, wait until your book's tech editing process has been completed before writing the front matter. In some instances, your TE's comments may influence the tone or other significant aspects of the book; you want the front matter to reflect the finished book, not the first draft, which could be quite different.

Writing the front matter is like spreading the icing on the cake. The icing completes the cake and makes it a thing of beauty; the cake's substance, essential as it is, is enhanced by the quality of that icing. I derive great joy from writing the front matter because, at this point, I know that the initial stages of my efforts are complete, and another manuscript is almost "in the can."

Keeping Track of Everything

In Chapter 4, in the section "Keeping Track of Your Work," I described the need to create a workbook consisting of worksheets you'll use to track the status of every chapter file, illustration, permission, and other details. Once you have submitted your draft chapters to the publisher, you'll begin to receive files that have been processed by the TE and later by the CE. In a typical tech book project, you'll be reviewing chapters returned to you after tech editing, then again after copy editing; at the same time, you'll be writing the first drafts of later chapters. At any given time, you may be juggling three, four, or more chapters in various stages of development simultaneously. This is where you need that very crisp recordkeeping so that you can track the precise status of every chapter file, every illustration, permissions for using illustrations and passages, and other details. You can't keep this all in your head.

The publisher expects you to be as organized as they are. This may feel like a tall task, but it's a reasonable one. The publisher's job is more complicated than yours, but yours is far from simple from a recordkeeping perspective. As you read through this chapter, you'll better understand the long and winding journey taken by your manuscript and the work performed by individuals who process your chapter files in various ways.

Using RACI to Track the Process

RACI, which stands for Responsible-Accountable-Consulted-Informed, is a notation businesses use to determine participants' involvement and responsibilities in a business process. The following example RACI shows who is responsible for what activities throughout a tech book's writing and revision processes.

	Author	Acquisitions Editor	Project Editor	Tech Editor	Copy Editor	Illustrator	Compositor	Proofreader	Marketing Staff
Write first draft	AR	I	C	I	I				
Coordinate overall project	I	AC	AR C						
Overall project success	AR	AR	AC						
Tech revisions	C	I	R	AR					
Review tech revisions	R	I	R	C					
Copy editing	C	I	R		AR				
Review copy editing	R	I	R						
Rough illustrations	R	I	R			CI			
Final illustrations	C	I	R			AR			
Review final illustrations	AR	I	R			C			
Obtain image permissions	AR	I	I						
Review image permissions	I	I	AR						
Page proofs	C	I	R				AR		
Review page proofs	AR	I	R				C		
Proofreading	C	I	R					AR	
Review proofreading	AR	I	AR						
Book promotion	AR	CI							CI

Key:
A: Accountable for the work
R: Responsible (generally the person who does the work)
C: Consulted (someone who reviews the work)
I: Informed (told about the work)

NOTE: I am not suggesting you establish a RACI with the publisher. The RACI chart here is designed to help you understand everyone's roles in the complete publishing project.

Tracking Edits

Most publishers use MS Word for manuscript development and editing. As of this writing, the browser-based version of Word lacks the full range of features required by authors and publishers. Hence, you will need to obtain a licensed copy of MS Word and install it on your computer.

Many publishers require that editors and authors use Word's Track Changes feature during the revision process. This reveals all the changes made in the document, including added and deleted text, and it identifies who made those changes. This helps the author easily find changes to check for accuracy, mistakes, queries, and other necessities.

Your publisher will probably have a policy about how you should deal with text changes, and this information will hopefully be included in an information packet you receive from the publisher. Most publishers will ask you not to accept or reject any changes during your review of edited chapters, and I strongly suggest that you follow their guidance. If you find a change to be acceptable, just leave it alone. If a change is unacceptable and the original text is correct, type in the correct text over the incorrect change, and this will appear as a new change, accredited to you. If you need to insert or change content, ensure that you use Track Changes so that everyone will see that this is new content that may require scrutiny.

As you review an edited chapter, you may notice that the editor has inserted some comments or queries in addition to general text edits. These comments can be inserted inline, or they may be inserted using Word's Comment feature. If you're lucky, your publisher will make this easier by including a style guide that indicates how to style or format comments to keep them separate from regular text. Or you have to make up your own method to differentiate these from regular edits.

For example, you may use a different font size or color for your comment, or you may insert comments and queries within brackets:

<<This is a comment or query for the author, from the copy editor, inside angle brackets.>>

> ```
> This example uses a different font and
> color for a question or comment to the
> author in the copy editing phase.
> ```

When you receive a revised chapter file from the PE, I recommend you save it and not work in the original file. Instead, make a copy of it and make your changes to the document. Use a consistent method for naming the document (I add "phg" at the end of the filename) to help you easily distinguish between the chapter from the PE and the document you are editing. Your publisher may offer you guidance on naming your reviewed files before sending them back to the PE.

You need to know something important about the revisions to your chapter files, whether these are from the TE, CE, PE, or proofreader: The changes you see are *suggestions* and are not mandatory. That said, you'll need to check your ego as you review edits and not take the changes personally, and it won't be in your best interest to refute every edit or complain to the PE if you disagree. Remember that everyone on the team is trying to make the book the best it can be, and nobody is trying to undermine you or your hard work.

Most of the editors working for established publishers are accomplished folks who do their jobs well. For this reason, it's usually safe to assume that you can allow their suggested changes to remain in the manuscript unless they distort what you are trying to say to the reader.

Most editors in tech publishing (and other forms of publishing) should know to respect an author's voice, but some may insert unnecessary changes that sound best to their own ear, rather than trusting the author's voice. Sometimes, a CE will "fix" a sentence in a way that may seem to read better, but at times this may inadvertently change the meaning from a technical point of view.

Copy editors are rarely SMEs in your book's domain, and they are not likely to be familiar with all of the vocabulary and/or common expressions used by you, other experts, or your readers. When making changes to a sentence or paragraph, astute CEs may insert a note to you, asking you to confirm that they have not distorted the meaning of a passage with their edits. However, even in the absence of such a note, it's your responsibility to ensure that every suggested change by any editor does not affect the fidelity of your content.

Working Through Revisions

The revision process is complicated, as several skilled professionals scrutinize every word, sentence, paragraph, and illustration in your book. The revision process is an absolute necessity for several reasons:

- **Consistency.** The publisher wants the book to be consistent with others they publish in terms of tone and appearance.
- **Quality.** As much expertise as you have in your technical domain, your content will include errors, even if you are a professional writer—some small and some not so small.
- **Reputation.** The publisher has a lot at stake when publishing a book. Readers have little tolerance for even minor errors, and with social media being what it is today, bad news travels fast and can have a potentially big impact.

The flow of your manuscript through the revision process is complex. Figure 8 depicts a generic workflow used by most of the publishers I work with. Of course, each publisher is a little (or a lot) different concerning how they progress through the editing and production stages, so you should be familiar with your publisher's practices.

If you are self-publishing, you should follow a similar process to ensure that your book is a quality work. I realize, of course, that if you're self-publishing, you are paying for all of the editing and other steps in this process. Rest assured, however, that it's worth the cost. Consider what could happen if too many errors appear in your book: who would trust your technical ability if the writing is poor, with misspellings, bad grammar, technical errors, and other issues that could have been found by following a detailed editing process? You do want people to trust you and buy your book, right?

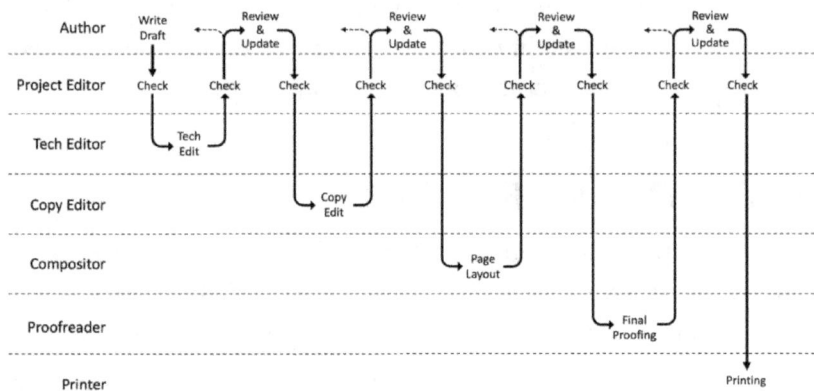

Figure 8. Typical manuscript revision workflow (source: author).

Note in the figure that each major step in the revision workflow shows a dotted arrow pointing backward, in addition to the forward-pointing arrows. This is because you may be asked to rework a chapter, which can happen at any stage of the process. And here is an example of why a thorough review process is essential. In one of my recent books, an attentive proofreader discovered that two paragraphs in one chapter appeared verbatim in another chapter. I missed this, the TE missed this, and the CE missed this. It happens! Unfortunately, this was caught late in the game, in page proofs, and one of the two chapters had to be sent back to me for some rewriting. After removing the duplicate content, I wrote some alternative content, which had to be copy edited and then sent back to the compositor, who had to redo a few page layouts. I tried to write replacement content that took approximately the same amount of space on the page; in this way, we avoided significant disruption in the page flows.

Roles and Responsibilities in the Revision Process

Each of the book's team members plays a vital role in the revision process. The following paragraphs are based on the procedures followed by most of the publishers I work with. However, keep in mind that not every publisher works in the same way, so you could be dealing with a completely different group of people with different roles and responsibilities.

Acquisitions Editor

The AE is not usually directly involved in the writing or revision processes, but this person will be kept aware of the book's progress. Generally, the AE will get involved if you aren't sticking to the writing schedule, if your writing reveals some egregious issues, if there is some sticky matter involving copyrights, or if the publisher is swapping people into or out of the project team.

Sometimes the PE will copy the AE in e-mail correspondence with you during the project (some AEs like to be highly involved in the details). Generally, I suggest you "reply all" to e-mails so that the AE is included in your replies to the PE; you want to reassure the AE that you are responsive and responsible.

Project Editor

As mentioned, the PE is the primary coordinator for the entire revision process. Unless you are directed to upload your content to a portal or a file hosting service such as Dropbox, you'll be transferring your chapter files, illustrations, photos, and other book matter to and from the PE via e-mail. Your PE will touch every chapter of your manuscript, every step of the way. From time to time, you may see edits made by the PE in addition to edits from others. Treat these edits as you would those of others.

Artists

After turning in your chapter drafts and graphical elements to the PE, all your photos, sketches, screenshots, and line art are sent to artists (aka illustrators), who will create camera-ready line art and adjust the size, contrast, and other factors in photographs. Unless an artist has trouble understanding what a final figure is supposed to look like, you won't usually see these figures again until page proofs.

Tech Editor

The TE has perhaps the most critical job in the entire revision process, because none of the other parties is capable of reviewing your content to ensure

- that your book is technically correct and includes no errors regarding the technology featured in your book,
- that references to external information sources, including URLs, are relevant and accurate,
- that your explanations for the use of technology represent a reasonable approach, and
- that your readers will understand and apply what you are telling them.

The TE is the last SME who will be scrutinizing your book, so the stakes for tech editing are high. A good TE must be critical and question everything. Anything less, and errors may creep in unnoticed—and CEs and proofreaders, who are not usually experts in the book's subject matter, probably won't catch them either.

In most situations, the TE will see the first draft of each chapter only once, unless you specifically ask the PE to send a chapter back to a TE to review your changes. (Note that a TE seeing your chapters a second time is not the norm but an exception. The publisher will send the chapter back to the TE only in unusual circumstances, such as your having added considerably more technical content.)

After the TE has reviewed a chapter, the PE will review the edits and then send the chapter to you. You'll need to read through the chapter carefully, noting and dealing with the TE's suggested changes and comments. I suggest you take the TE's suggestions and comments seriously. Do not, however, count on the TE having confirmed every fact in your book; that's your job. You always need to keep a careful eye out for any errors you may have made that other editors don't catch.

When reviewing your manuscript, some TEs will insert a comment such as, "You forgot about this or that." More thorough editors may jump right in and add the missing content. When a TE inserts technical content, you and the TE are switching roles, and you'll be reviewing their additions.

As always, bring a healthy dose of humility to this stage. Although you are the author, you are not the most intelligent person on the planet, and your TE, who may know more than you in many areas, might have numerous suggestions that will make the book far better. As mentioned earlier, your success depends on your ability to work with the rest of the team to create the best book possible.

If you selected the TE for your book, I suggest you have one or more live conversations before the start of the actual tech editing so that the two of you are of one mind regarding the book's purpose, flow, and tone. If you did not select the TE, ask the AE or the PE to introduce you so you can have that live conversation. Being connected with your TE enables you to correspond with this person as you write your book and as they review each chapter. This connection can add considerable value and effectiveness to the tech editing process, taking less time than it would if you did not connect.

Copy Editor

After you have reviewed the work performed by the TE, you'll send the chapter back to the PE, who will clean up the manuscript and forward it to the CE. Copy editors look for readability, voice, grammar, punctuation, spelling, consistency issues (called "style" in publishing), and more. Depending upon your writing style and how it differs from the tone and style required by the publisher, you may see a few—or numerous—edits by your CE.

Copy editors are language experts, and their work will result in your book being more readable. They are probably not experts in the book's subject matter, however, so it's essential that you carefully review each change to ensure that the CE has not inadvertently distorted what you intended to say.

Here's an example of how this might happen. In a book about information systems auditing, suppose you've written, "Internal audit must be mindful of the controls in place and develop an audit plan accordingly." Your CE may decide that "safeguards" is a better word than "controls," unaware that "controls" is a specific industry term that should not be changed. Although, in a generic sense, "safeguards" may make the sentence read better, "controls" is the technical term that must remain.

Some CE edits will be more subtle. It's never safe for you to assume that the CE's changes are correct. Instead, you must read through each change to ensure that the fidelity of your explanations has not been changed. Often, if a CE recognizes that a change may inadvertently affect the meaning of a passage, they will insert an inline note to you to double-check the work. The absence of such a note does not automatically mean that a change is appropriate, however. Check each edit carefully.

Like a TE's edits, a CE's edits are suggestions (except in the case of grammar, misspellings, and similar finite issues), but I recommend that you go with most of their changes. Your publisher may ask you not to "accept" the favorable changes in Track Changes, because the PE will do this, so you must leave them be. If you disagree with a change, do not "reject" the change; instead, rewrite over the edit using the language you want. Or leave a short note explaining why the edit is incorrect.

As you review the CE edits, remember that *this is your last opportunity to make significant changes to your manuscript.* And keep in mind that if you make significant changes after the CE has edited the manuscript, those changes will have to go back to the CE again for review, which can add time to the schedule.

Although you and the AE, TE, and PE will communicate via e-mail or other means, you probably won't communicate directly with the CE. Usually, any issues encountered by the CE that need attention are forwarded to the PE or AE, who will contact you directly. Copy editors are often freelance consultants; because they are not directly employed by the publisher, they usually do not contact authors. This is left up to full-time staff, when possible.

After you turn in your review of the copy edited chapters to the PE, the PE will clean up ("accept") all the edits, remove inline comments, and bring your chapter file into a state that is ready for the compositor.

Compositor

After the PE cleans up the chapter file, it is sent to a compositor to create page proofs, the draft version of how your book will look in print. The compositor will perform several steps:

- Flow Word text into design software
- Add page headers and footers, including page numbers
- Apply fonts and styles, according to the book's design
- Insert completed illustrations, photographs, and other art
- Transform tables and similar elements into their final form and style
- Lay out the pages by determining the best places to insert page breaks

When the compositor completes the book's layout, the PE sends you PDFs of the page proofs. These proofs are also sent to the proofreader and the indexer, either electronically or in hard copy (or sometimes both).

Generally, you will be directed to review the following:

- Correct section headings at the appropriate heading levels

- Check that images and graphical elements are inserted in the appropriate places (because of layout issues, tables and illustrations may appear a bit ahead of or behind the placeholders you include in your manuscript)
- Correct formatting of sidebars, bulleted lists, tables, formulas, excerpts, and so forth

You will likely be asked to insert comments and other content into the PDFs using Adobe Acrobat Reader. You should not make changes directly in the PDF files, because the compositor will not see what changes you made.

Look for errors that were not detected earlier. You can make minor changes to the page proofs, provided they do not affect the page flows (where the compositor has determined that page breaks should occur). Because page breaks can change the page count (if a change results in more or fewer pages), and because the indexer is also looking at page proofs to create the index, generally speaking, you should avoid making *any* changes at this point.

If you find an egregious problem, ideally, any addition should result in no more than one or two additional lines of text, and you should remove no more than one or two lines to avoid page flow issues. Compositors can usually adjust the type to maintain a page break that occurs with a minor change. If, however, you make changes that involve more than two lines of text, the compositor may have to reflow a part of, or the entire, chapter. That will take extra time, and time is money. The publisher will find it annoying if you make more extensive changes at this stage; in fact, your changes may be ignored at page proofs unless they are absolutely necessary. Recall that I mentioned that your copy editing review is your last chance to make significant changes.

Proofreader

The proofreader will also review the PDF chapter files, or they may be sent printouts of the page proofs. The proofreader will carefully look over the content, making any final spelling, grammatical, text styling, and other similar edits. The proofreader also checks page and figure numbering, headers and footers, margins, and other layout issues.

After the PE reviews the proofreader's marks, they will send you chapter PDFs with the proofreader's comments so that you can approve any changes made.

Indexer

Most publishers use professional indexers to create indexes for their books, and most indexers are freelance contractors. The indexer works from the PDFs of page proofs while you and the proofreader are viewing them. I have found that the indexers used by my tech publishers are proficient and accurate; I cannot recall seeing outright errors in any of my books' indexes. You may ask the publisher to let you review the index, but I caution you not to be too critical if you have the opportunity; it may not be a good use of your time. I suggest you trust experienced indexers to do their work. You can take a look at the index when your bound book copies arrive at your door.

Book Designer

As mentioned earlier, the book designer determines the visual aspects of the book—the page layouts, including the fonts used, book trim, and other aspects of the book design. They also design the book's cover.

Most publishers will ask you to review the draft and final versions of the front and back covers, spine, and inside cover elements. Make sure that you take the opportunity to review the draft cover to ensure that everything is correct. Two of my early books had errors on their covers—specifically, both listed my certifications incorrectly, and one book showed my name incorrectly. If you have the opportunity to review cover content, note that the publisher may require a very rapid, even same-day, turnaround because of printing scheduling concerns. Be prepared to be as responsive as the publisher needs.

Marketing Staff

Publishers market their books on their websites and those of major book retailers such as Amazon, Barnes & Noble, and others. The publisher will probably borrow descriptions of your book from your proposal, from the book itself, or other existing content. If you have the opportunity to review promotional content before its release, it can't hurt. Just be sure to be as responsive as the publisher requires. If you don't have an opportunity to review draft copies of promotional content that will appear on these websites, visit the sites to look at them. If you see any errors, let your PE know as soon as possible.

6 AFTER PUBLICATION

Few things in life bring satisfaction and joy like the completion and publication of a book that you've authored. While a celebration may be called for, your work isn't done yet—the work transitions from the creation and production of the book to the promotion of the book. Whether you're trying to make as much money as possible or reach as many readers as possible, it helps if you can shift your efforts to promotion to get your book out there to promote sales.

Celebrate!

This is the time to celebrate. You worked hard on this book—perhaps a lot harder than initially imagined. You may have worked harder writing your book than you worked to earn a master's degree, for instance. Although it's appropriate to celebrate, I'm not going to tell you how—that's up to you. Whether you have friends over, go out to dinner, have a virtual happy hour with people who helped on the book, or give thanks to God, be sure to celebrate that the creative part of your book is finished.

Unboxing Your Books

As the author, you are entitled to receive several free copies of your book from the publisher. This is stipulated in your contract. Usually, these books show up at your door a week or so before the books are available online or in bookstores. Consider these copies the "first fruit" that resulted from a successful project.

There's nothing quite like the unboxing process. I won't attempt to describe the elation you'll feel when you see the first bound book. I often literally take a photo of the box as soon as I open it, even before I take a book out of the box to look it over.

Figure 9. The unboxing of a recent book written by the author (source: author).

Distributing Copies

I've made it a custom to send copies of my new books to the TEs and others who contributed to their quality. I write a nice note of thanks to each recipient on the title page, and I pay for the postage (I can write it off as a business expense). If your family members (parents, children, siblings) are some of your biggest supporters, consider giving them copies, with notes of thanks for their support.

Keep two copies for yourself: one that is pristine and unopened, and another for referencing errata, which can also be used as a reference if your book warrants another edition. If you still have copies left over, don't fret—you'll find opportunities to give copies to well-deserving people:

- Your boss, if this person is a fan
- People you mentor, if they want to learn more about the technology focus of your book
- Social media influencers who value their relationship with you (or vice versa)

Over many years, even after giving away copies, I had accumulated more than 100 copies of various published books that I've authored. With help from a colleague, after I found a nonprofit that focuses on helping women start cybersecurity careers, I shipped all the books to the organization with my compliments.

Promoting Your Book

Your book's publisher will not lease billboard space or take out TV or radio advertisements to promote your book. All promotion will be done by the sweat of your brow. While I'm experienced at promoting my books, I don't consider myself an expert, as book promotion is outside my core competency. Still, I know what I know, and I know what I don't know about book promotion. This section offers some ideas for generating publicity and getting the word out about your book. You'll likely want to read more about this from additional sources.

Soliciting Reviews

Your book's success relies heavily upon its ratings and reviews on Amazon.com and other online booksellers' sites to a lesser extent. For this reason, you should strategically and intentionally rely on getting some good, early reviews of your book posted on the Amazon site and elsewhere. Ask professional associates if they are willing to write a review. Offer them a copy of the book to reference, unless they have already purchased one of their own.

Posting on Social Media

I presume you have a profile on LinkedIn, the king of professional social networking sites. If not, this is a perfect time to sign up. LinkedIn is a great place to promote your book, where your professional connections and others can learn of its release:

- Once the book is mentioned on Amazon.com or the publisher's website, write a post that announces that the book will be published.
- Post your unboxing photo to announce the book's completion and availability.
- Coordinate with the publisher to set up a book giveaway promotion.

Blogging and Building a Community

If you're a published author, consider blogging about professional topics to help readers learn more about you and your book. I've been blogging for years, although I'll admit that I slowed down somewhat when I started posting on Twitter and LinkedIn. Recently, however, I've turned my focus to strategic LinkedIn postings, and I'm blogging more. On my blog, I've been posting short articles on various topics relevant to my profession, as well as short book excerpts.

> **NOTE:** While I'm on the subject of book excerpts, I recommend that you have a conversation with your AE to see what the publisher considers reasonable for the length or number of excerpts you'll be posting. You want to post enough to generate interest in your book, but you don't want to put the entire book out there in pieces.

Offering a Free Chapter

Talk with your AE about giving away a free chapter of your book. Your publisher can create a PDF with a cover page, complete TOC, and one of your book chapters. Then, through manual or automatic means, you can send a PDF chapter to anyone who asks for it. You could even add a download link for the free chapter on your blog site or LinkedIn profile. I like to give people a free chapter in exchange for joining my blog feed.

Speaking Engagements

If you are booked for a speaking engagement, this is a perfect opportunity to promote your talk and your book. And you can help lift attendance to your talk by promoting it on social media.

I've been a frequent industry conference speaker since the late 1990s. My biggest year was 2016, when I keynoted one conference and spoke at twelve other industry conferences (including two in one day, one in Las Vegas and another in Albuquerque). I have one or two "About the Speaker" slides that I briefly show at each presentation. On another slide, I show cover images of many of my books or just a few recent releases.

I often give away a few copies of my books in my talks. My method is this: My talks are very interactive, and I give away copies of books to people who ask particularly good questions. This helps get the audience engaged, making for a better conversation, more learning on the part of attendees, and a bit of free publicity for my books.

Book Signing

Once a popular way of promoting sales, book signings aren't that hot anymore. There is another avenue available, however: doing a book signing at an industry conference. I've seen them and done them. At an industry conference, you have a captive audience of like-minded professionals who are there to learn about the same or related technologies.

There are two ways to go about a conference book signing: Asking the conference organizer to feature your book signing is the best way to go because your signing will be on the conference schedule or will be featured somehow. If the conference organizer won't promote your book signing, you can still do a signing by promoting it yourself on

LinkedIn and other social media. Just use hashtags that will get conference attendees' attention.

At my conference book signings, I didn't have a long line of followers, but I did meet many interesting people, some of whom I still correspond with. You never know who you'll meet at a book signing or where that chance meeting will take you in the future.

Book Promoters

Some legitimate professionals and companies will take care of your book promotion and publicity. Naturally, there is a fee involved. Promoters offer various services to promote your book. I suggest you talk with different promoters, and speak with some of their customers; better promoters will have references or give you some contact information for some of their author clients.

Full disclosure: I have not used a book promoter, and it's my perception that professional promoters do a better job of it than I could. And busy writers may not want to take the time required to promote our books constantly.

Dealing with Errata

It is said that a book's readers perform the final QA of a manuscript. Regardless of the publishing team's effort to ensure the final manuscript's quality and accuracy, errors can creep in, and you can count on your readers to find them for you. If your book's quality processes were effective, however, there should be few errors—perhaps a typo or maybe a technical fact that is not quite right.

You'll learn about errors in several ways:
- Reader reviews on book retailers' websites will mention egregious errors.
- Readers may contact you directly.
- You may spot errors yourself.

I suggest you keep a formal record of errata found in your book. In your tracking, note how the error was discovered (retain the contact info of the person who found it, if applicable) and whether you informed the publisher of the error. If you someday write a second edition, you'll want to use your errata records to ensure that errors are corrected in the next edition. Of course, new errors will probably creep into the next edition, too, so be sure to start your recordkeeping cycle over again.

Today's social media phenomena and product reviews can work against you if your book contains errors. Your reviews will suffer if too many errors are found, which could significantly dampen your book's sales.

If you do spot any errors, do not panic. Published books often contain errors despite our best efforts, and there are a few remedies available:

- **Errata page on publisher's site.** Publishers often will include a link to an errata page on your book's web page, which can be updated as frequently as required.
- **Errata page on your book's promotion site.** Same story; add a link.
- **Reprints.** If your book sells a significant number of hard copies, the publisher can ask for minor revisions to be made to ensure that these errors are absent in subsequent printings. Most publishers will agree to make changes if they do not affect more than the page where the error occurred. Publishers are less likely to make changes that affect page flows or page counts in a reprint.
- **E-books.** You should be able to make corrections quickly to the contents of an e-book so that subsequently sold copies reflect the corrections.

Pirate Sites

You might be surprised to know that numerous download sites will promote free PDF copies of your book. This practice is a clear case of copyright violation and a thorn in the publisher's side, because these sites are stealing from you and the publisher.

In one of your conversations with your AE, bring up the subject of bootleg book downloads to learn how your publisher handles these. Your AE may give you the name of a contact in the publishing company who issues takedown requests or even takes legal action against site owners.

I learn about pirate sites through automated search services that alert me to new sites that feature my name or book titles. I get monthly search results for new appearances on the web, and every month this includes one or more bootleg download sites. I send these URLs to my publishers, who do whatever they do to reduce pirate market sales. The search services I use are Google Alerts at google.com/alerts and Giga Alerts at gigaalert.com.

7 WRITING SUBSEQUENT EDITIONS

Technical books have short shelf lives. Because of the pace of innovation and changes in technology, a tech book will become outdated faster than nonfiction books on other topics, such as gardening or home repair. You are fortunate indeed if you have an opportunity to revise your book and write a second edition. That your publisher is asking you to author another edition is a statement that your first edition was a commercial success and that the topic is still relevant.

Be sure to understand the difference between a second *edition* and a second *printing*. A second edition is a separate publication from the first edition. A second (or third, fourth, and so on) edition involves a process of making minor and/or major changes to the manuscript and publishing it under a new ISBN. A second printing is the manufacture (literally, printing) of more copies of a book for sale. Because printing books is expensive, a publisher won't print too many copies of the first edition; they don't want to destroy the surplus if the books don't sell. It's better to print fewer books and schedule a second print run (of the same book) a year or two later.

For me, writing a second edition takes less overall effort than writing the first edition. In a first edition, you're writing from scratch, whereas in second and subsequent editions, you're making changes and improvements to an already existing manuscript.

Contract Addendums

Once you and the publisher have verbally agreed that you will write a second (or subsequent) edition, the publisher will send you a contract addendum. Generally, the contract for the first edition will still prevail; the addendum is an update to that contract, describing the new, second edition. The contract addendum will reference the original contract, including copyrights, royalty rates, advance payments, page count, table of contents, and schedule.

If you have a literary agent, your agent will negotiate the terms for you. Still, you need to read, understand, and agree to the terms. Your agent will help you get better rates and terms, but in the end, it's your book and your signature on the contract.

Research for Subsequent Editions

Your tech book is going into a second edition for one of several reasons:

- Updated technical standards
- Updated products related to the technology
- Updated techniques, processes, and procedures for using the technology
- Newly identified threats to the technology
- New regulations that apply to the technology
- New quality, security, privacy, or resilience standards that apply to the technology

As the author of your tech book, naturally, you need to be familiar with whatever changes drive the business justification for a revision. The publisher may require a detailed account of these changes and how you will incorporate them into the next edition.

Unless you work every day in the changing technology, the research you need to conduct may take quite a bit of time and effort. You may need to obtain updated technical standards, product manufacturer specifications, copies of appropriate laws and regulations, relevant news articles, and more. It may be necessary for you to interview SMEs to become more familiar with the impact and consequences of changes. Finally, you may need to observe the technology directly to get the insight necessary to impart wisdom to your readers.

Who drives the need for a second edition? If the publisher reaches out to you, it means that they have learned about some things you need to understand and validate in a new edition. If your research or work compels you to pitch the idea to the publisher, you may need to deepen your research to gather enough meaningful details about updates and changes to convince them to publish a new edition.

Research Records

In Chapter 4, I provided pointers on the detailed records you'll need to track the minutiae of your book. Similarly, you'll benefit from a detailed workbook where you chronicle new research, which contains the following:

- Web pages you've read, with URLs
- Sources for every article, whitepaper, specification, or standard you consult
- Correspondence with others
- Conversations with others, with details on information sources
- Charts and tables to compare changes in specs, standards, laws, practices, and so on
- Things you want to explore for a new edition

Over many years, my writing has fit firmly within the niche of cybersecurity, privacy, and business continuity, often associated with prestigious industry certifications. For me, research for subsequent editions consists of three phases:

1. Changes in certification knowledge/experience requirements
2. Changes in business processes, techniques, approaches

3. Changes in technologies and uses of technologies

The first item is defined by the certification body itself. The other two are solely my responsibility to identify. Often, I'm familiar with the nature of the second two items through my daily work, although I strive to reach out to others to learn more and confirm my suspicions.

After your research is completed and your writing has begun, you'll often find that you need to know even more as you write out the details of any of the new technologies or practices you've discovered in your research. This is where detailed records will help you. Instead of hunting through e-mails or other notes, you can reference only your research notes and their citations. To learn more, follow the breadcrumbs you left behind and delve into even greater detail. If you do not keep detailed research notes, you're going to waste much time looking here and there in a vain attempt to pick up where you think you left off.

The Revision Process

The end-to-end process of writing a second edition is similar to that of the first. You're still producing chapter files, which are processed by TEs, CEs, compositors, and proofreaders, and the PE still tracks everything and keeps the project flowing. You're likely to be adding and updating figures as well. Everything I describe in detail in Chapter 4 takes place in subsequent editions.

One big difference is this: The publisher will send you a set of chapter files from the previous edition, cleaned up and ready for you to revise. These will be in the same format used for manuscript files in the previous edition, such as MS Word or Google Docs.

If the publisher does not provide a clean set of chapter files, you'll need to do your best to clean up the final copy-edited chapters (did I mention you need to save these from the last edition?) and then look up and apply changes made in the page proof reviews and proofreading. This cleanup will take a bit of time. You must start with precisely what was published in the first edition; the second edition must reflect every correction made to the first. Some (or much) of your first edition content will appear in the completed second edition, and you don't want to be pulling uncorrected errors into the second edition.

TOC Revisions

Your second edition's overall structure, including the TOC, may need to change if the technology has changed substantially. Or, perhaps as or after you wrote the first edition, you've come up with better ways of structuring your book. Your book's second edition could provide an opportunity to make those necessary changes. The same rules for TOC structure and changes that applied to the first edition apply to the second: If you need to make changes to the TOC, you need to clear this with the AE and/or PE, who may send the revised TOC to one or more outside SMEs for their opinion.

Restructuring

The degree of change you make from one edition to the next can vary quite a lot. In some editions, you may be making hundreds of minor changes, adding and deleting paragraphs here and there and updating a few figures.

You may need to make significant changes in some editions, however, which could include changing the number of chapters and their focus. I've experienced a few major edition updates like this. For these, I've marked groups of paragraphs and entire sections for deletion, restructured sections, built new chapters out of pieces from many other chapters, and wrote a lot of new content.

Your ability to complete a book's restructuring requires three things:

- Long spans of quiet time
- A good plan for tracking the big changes
- A consistent method for making the big changes without making mistakes

Manuscript restructuring is a broader undertaking than rearranging your sock drawer; it's more like emptying your entire garage, putting in new storage systems (shelves, racks, cabinets, and so on), and putting everything back in an entirely different and more logical way. You still have all the same stuff (mostly, although you probably found some things to discard), but it's arranged differently—and, hopefully, better.

Revision Page Count

You and the publisher must agree on the page count of your second edition. Generally, either your page count target is the same, which means you'll carefully track the amount of additional content you write and find other sections to shorten to retain the page count, or the publisher will agree to a higher page count with a correspondingly higher retail price tag. Page count is a matter to work out before the contract addendum is signed; after that, the publisher will not likely agree to a significant change.

Even if the page count target is the same in your second edition, the publisher may budget for one, or even two, additional book *signatures*. Printers create signatures to lay out book pages on a large press sheet so that, after folding and cutting, they are in the correct order. Depending on the publisher, the book's dimensions, and the printer, a signature can equal 8, 16, or 32 pages. Before you start your revisions, it's essential to understand the publisher's parameters and expectations for your second edition's final page count.

Applying Fixes

Recall that you and the proofreader will have made some changes in the page proofs of your book's previous edition. Check with the PE to determine whether those changes are reflected in your clean chapter files or whether you need to reapply them yourself. Similarly, if you applied corrections for subsequent print runs in your previous edition, those corrections will not be reflected in the original edition's chapter files.

Before you start work on your new edition, you should also refer to the Errata tab in your prior edition workbook to check for errors you want to correct in the new edition. In addition, read your book's reviews on Amazon, Barnes & Noble, your publisher's website, and other places where readers will have made helpful (and some not too helpful) comments on your previous edition. Consider fixing all errors cited, and consider other feedback that may compel you to make further changes.

Existing and New Illustrations

If you're working on a pre-page proof copy of your manuscript from your first edition (such as the MS Word file), the chapters will include only the placeholders for illustrations, not the illustrations themselves (just as your original and edited chapter files did in the first edition). You can refer to the corresponding page proofs to view the illustrations or use a hard copy of the first edition book to follow along and determine what illustrations appeared in the first edition and whether any of those need to be removed or replaced in the second edition.

If you drew rough sketches for your first edition line art and any need to be updated, I suggest you print copies of the original sketches, indicating any necessary changes on each copy. The publisher almost certainly has retained the original sketches, and one of their artists can apply the needed changes for the second edition.

You may be writing your second edition because of changes to software programs. In this case, you'll need to reshoot your screen images. If the OS is apparent in any of these screenshots, make sure it is up-to-date with the latest patches. Your images all need to appear *current*, not outdated. For example, if your first edition had some whole-screen images and you were running Windows XP or Windows 7, you'll want to reshoot them running Windows 10 or Windows 11.

Updating Content

If you are asked to work on a clean set of first-edition manuscript chapters, I strongly suggest that, before you start inserting or deleting material, you turn on Track Changes (in MS Word) to see the additions, changes, and deletions you make. Your revisions will be highlighted in the manuscript, which is incredibly helpful to those working on the second edition. The chapter files sent to the TE must include the tracked notations so that the TE can pay specific attention to what you changed (and less attention to what you didn't change).

Your TE will also be familiar with changes in standards, products, techniques that occurred between the first edition and the second. As the author, you may be revered as an authoritative source of all knowledge related to your book's subject matter, and you may indeed possess considerable knowledge—but you probably don't know everything. Your TE will likely identify any changes that you may have overlooked and can either suggest you include these changes or make the changes him- or herself. This is tech editing at its best.

As with the first edition, you might have a say in selecting the TE for your second edition. You may want to work with the same person, who will be quite knowledgeable about your book's subject matter. There could be an advantage to bringing in a new TE for the second edition, however. Because so few experts have an opportunity to read and update your manuscript before publication, having a new TE review your second edition brings in potentially new knowledge and perspectives that can make this edition even better.

Adding a Preface

You may decide to write a preface that explains the nature of the second edition, where you describe changes in standards, protocols, techniques, products, practices, and other appropriate details. You can add remarks about insights you learned in your research, including the implications of new information included in this edition.

Changing the Cover

As with the first edition, you should have an opportunity to review the rough and final cover layouts for your second edition. Make sure that any descriptions of the content reflect the current practices that are the focus of the second edition. If the book includes any "about the author" content, be sure it is up-to-date as well.

Language Translations

Some of the fine print in your publishing contract will address the royalties you will receive for language translations. If your book sells well and speaks to a broad audience beyond U.S. shores and borders, it may appear in other languages.

In terms of logistics, there's nothing for you to do regarding the translation of your book into another language. The publisher will commission the translation, undergo a similar review process, and publish your book. The translation could happen without your awareness unless your AE happens to inform you about it. If you read your royalty statements carefully, you may spot sales numbers associated with translated editions.

Publishers often employ outside companies to complete the translation process, and sometimes you will not receive personal copies of translations. My first book, *Solaris Security*, was translated into Chinese and Japanese. For the Chinese edition, the publisher sent me two copies. To obtain the Japanese edition, I had to log on to Amazon.co.jp, navigate the Japanese Amazon site (following along with another window open in Amazon.com in English), and purchase two copies that Amazon Japan shipped to me.

Figure 10. Japanese language edition of my first book (source: Solaris Security, Japanese Language edition; Prentice-Hall, publisher).

REFERENCES AND RESOURCES

Curtis, Richard. *How to Be Your Own Literary Agent: An Insider's Guide to Getting Your Book Published*, 3rd Edition. 2003. Houghton Mifflin Company. Insightful, detailed advice on negotiating contracts. This book provides background on what your literary agent does for you; recommended even if you don't have a literary agent.

Larsen, Michael. *Literary Agents: What They Do, How They Do It, and How to Find and Work with the Right One for You*, 1st Edition. 1996. Wiley Publishing. Despite its low Amazon.com ratings, I found this book highly insightful in the early stages of my writing career.

Peterson, Chris. *Home Office Solutions: How to Set Up an Efficient Workspace Anywhere in Your House*, 1st Edition. 2020. Creative Homeowner. Ideas for establishing or improving your writing space.

Strunk, William Jr. *The Elements of Style: Annotated Edition*. 2020. Auroch Press. An abbreviated, concise style guide to writing.

The University of Chicago Press Editorial Staff. *The Chicago Manual of Style*, 17th Edition. 2017. University of Chicago Press. The writer's bible for writing style, including every sort of topic imaginable.

Writing, Publishing, and Reference Tools

- **Adobe FrameMaker publishing software:** www.adobe.com/products/framemaker.html
- **Calmly Writer:** calmlywriter.com
- **Dragon Home speech recognition software:** nuance.com/dragon/dragon-for-pc/home-edition.html
- **Evernote:** evernote.com
- **Giga Alerts:** www.gigaalert.com
- **Google Alerts:** google.com/alerts
- **Google Docs:** docs.google.com
- **Grammarly Pro writing assistant software:** grammarly.com
- **Leanpub authoring:** leanpub.com
- **LibreOffice office suite (formerly Open Office):** libreoffice.org
- **Mendeley Reference Manager:** www.mendeley.com
- **Microsoft Office productivity software:** office.com
- **Pro Writing Aid:** prowritingaid.com
- **Reedsy authoring:** reedsy.com
- **Scrivener authoring tool:** scrivener.app
- **Snagit screenshot tool:** techsmith.com/store/snagit
- **Wikimedia Commons media file repository:** commons.wikimedia.org

Book Promotion

- **Facebook:** facebook.com
- **Instagram:** instagram.com
- **LinkedIn:** linkedin.com
- **Twitter:** twitter.com

E-book Publishers

- **Barnes & Noble Press:** press.barnesandnoble.com
- **Draft 2 Digital:** draft2digital.com
- **Kindle Direct Publishing:** kdp.amazon.com
- **Leanpub:** leanpub.com
- **Lulu Press:** lulu.com
- **Scribd:** scribd.com/publishers
- **Smashwords:** smashwords.com/about/how_to_publish_on_smashwords

GLOSSARY

about the author A short biography of the author and any co-authors that may appear in the front matter or back matter.

acquisitions editor (AE) An executive at a publishing company who negotiates a book contract with an author and oversees the overall publishing process.

addendum The publisher's additional contractual elements of a subsequent edition of a book.

advance Cash paid up front to the author as an inducement to write a manuscript; considered prepaid royalties.

agent *See* literary agent.

agreement *See* publishing agreement.

air gap A technical term used to describe the physical separation between environments. In writing, refers to the separation between an author's day job and his or her professional writing work.

artist A role in the publishing process responsible for creating line art and formatting photographs for use in a book. Also referred to as an illustrator.

attribution A formal acknowledgment of the owner and source of an image, figure, or other content to be included in a book.

audience The readers of your book, including persons working in specific industries or persons in companies with particular job titles.

Glossary

back matter Content that appears at the back of the book, such as appendixes, references, endnotes, and the index.

backup The copies of your book files kept to protect them in the event of an incident resulting in the loss of your files, or the process of making those copies. It is suggested that you keep some backup copies nearby if you need to recover files, but that you also keep copies far away in the event of a fire, flood, or theft.

basket accounting A technique used by publishers in which the royalties for a successful book are used to earn back the advance for a previous, less successful book.

book weight A desk object that holds a book open, enabling the open pages to be read hands-free.

camera ready A term used to signify that book manuscript pages or images have been prepared and are ready to be sent to a printer.

co-author A person who shares the role of authoring a single book or article.

competing title A published book on the same or a similar topic as a book being proposed for publication.

compositor A person who uses software to transform a book manuscript, often created in MS Word, into its final, camera-ready form for printing.

contract A binding legal agreement between two or more parties. *See also* publishing agreement.

copy editor (CE) An editor who is responsible for correcting grammatical, punctuation, voice, style, and formatting errors.

copyright A legal claim on a published work, such as an illustration, article, recording, or book.

copyright page A page in a book's front matter that includes information about the publisher, author, significant contributors, a copyright statement, the ISBN, and other information.

draft The first or early version manuscript of a chapter or an entire book.

earned out   The state of book royalty earnings in which the royalty amount has exceeded the advance paid to the author.

e-book   A book published in an electronic format.

errata   Corrections to a published book, whether listed on a slip of paper inserted into the book after printing or on a website.

figure   A numbered image included in a book, which may be line art, a photograph, or a screenshot.

foreword   Front matter content that precedes the main body of a book; it is usually written by someone other than the author.

front matter   Content that appears in the front of a book, which may include the title page, subtitle page, copyright page, table of contents, about the author section, acknowledgments, dedication, preface, and foreword.

glossary   A section of a book that offers formal definitions for terms used in the book, usually found at or near the end of the book.

illustration   A graphical image included in a book, which may be line art, a photograph, or a screenshot.

index   A section in a book's back matter that lists key words and concepts and the associated page numbers where these are defined or used.

indexer   A person who creates an index for a book.

intellectual property   Intangible creations of the human intellect. Also, a category of laws that protect such creations.

line art   Simple drawings made with distinct straight and curved lines, along with labels. Examples of line art include simple schematics, flowcharts, and Venn diagrams.

list of illustrations   A detailed list of the illustrations and photographs included in a book, along with their associated page numbers.

list of tables   A detailed list of the tables contained in a book, along with their associated titles and page numbers.

Glossary

literary agent An individual who is paid, usually a percentage of the author's royalties, to acquire and manage publishing contracts on behalf of an author.

manuscript The complete set of chapter files and other content to be published as a book.

market study Research performed to determine the economic feasibility of developing and selling a product such as a book.

markup Visible editing within a manuscript that consists of suggested changes and comments, such as the marks created using Track Changes in MS Word.

moiré pattern A distracting pattern that appears in printed material when an image is created by overlaying two or more patterned images; often occurs in printed photographs of television screens or computer monitors.

nondisclosure agreement (NDA) A legal, signed agreement in which two or more parties agree to keep secret certain proprietary elements for a specific period of time.

page count The number of pages in a camera-ready chapter, section, or book; also, the number of pages expected to be included in the book, mentioned in the book proposal.

page flow A book's page-by-page appearance in page proofs—the final, camera-ready form—including the placement of illustrations, section headings, and page breaks.

page proof The camera-ready book manuscript created by a compositor. The author, PE, and proofreader usually view PDFs of the page proofs to search for last-minute errors, and the indexer uses the page proofs to create the book's index. Fixing errors at this stage can cost the publisher time and money.

permission Formal consent required to use the intellectual property of another person or entity within a book or article.

plagiarism The act of appropriating content from another party without permission.

preface An introduction to the book, written by the author, that appears in the front matter.

project editor (PE) A role in the publishing process that is responsible for managing the workflow of manuscript creation, editing, and production.

proofreading The final inspection of a manuscript at page proofs, prior to printing.

proposal A formal document created by an author that makes a business case for publishing a book on a particular topic.

publishing agreement A binding legal agreement between a publisher and one or more authors, stating the terms for creation of a book, its publication, ownership of copyrights, and payments to author(s).

rights Intellectual property rights, such as copyrights, trademarks, and patents.

royalties Financial compensation to the author resulting from the sale of copies of a book. Royalties may be calculated on a percentage of sales basis or a fixed amount per copy sold.

second edition A subsequent and separate release of a book that contains additions and revisions to the first edition.

second printing A subsequent printing of a book to increase inventories. Minor corrections can be applied to second and subsequent printings.

self-publishing A publishing arrangement in which an author assumes the role of publisher.

shelf life The span of time during which a book's subject matter will be relevant.

signature A unit representing 4, 8, 16, or 32 pages of a published book; created by printers to lay out book pages on a large press sheet so that after folding and cutting they are in the correct order.

surge protector An electronic device that passes electrical current to a number of other devices plugged into it to protect electrical devices from potentially harmful anomalies such as voltage spikes and surges.

table of contents (TOC) A detailed and chronological listing of heading levels used in a book, along with page numbers corresponding to each chapter and/or section location.

technical editor (TE) A role in the publishing process responsible for reviewing the technical content of a book to ensure its accuracy, completeness, and logic. A TE, sometimes known as a technical reviewer, is a subject matter expert on the topic of the book.

template A manuscript document attachment that contains page layout, formatting, and styles; often MS Word .dot files.

title The name of a published book that appears on the cover.

title page The page in the front matter that includes the book's title, author, publisher, and edition.

touch typing A style of typing in which the typist need not look at the keyboard.

Track Changes A feature of MS Word by which revisions to a document are tracked and visually indicated and attributed for clarity.

trademark A type of intellectual property that consists of a recognizable design that distinguishes one organization's product from others.

uninterruptible power supply (UPS) An appliance that provides continuous power in the event of a utility power failure.

vanity publishing A publishing arrangement in which an author pays a publisher to publish a book, regardless of its market value.

work for hire An arrangement wherein an individual performs work on a fixed-fee basis as opposed to a royalty basis.

working title A preliminary title for a book.

writer's block A psychological condition in which a writer is unable to continue to produce content.

INDEX

A

acquisitions editor, 52, 115
advance, 11, 37, 44
agent. *See* literary agent
artist, 55, 116
attribution, 27, 46
audience, 13, 28
author qualifications, 24

B

backup, 98
basket accounting. *See* royalties
book format, 34, 36, 76

C

co-author, 25, 42, 51, 94–96
code of conduct, 61
color, 88
competing titles, 30
compositor, 56, 119
computer, 66
content protection, 97–99
contract, 41
 addendum, 132
copy editor, 54, 117
copyright, 42, 47–50
cover, book, 139

D

data storage, 67
dictation, 19

disk encryption, 101

E

employer, 60–63
errata, 128–29
ethics. *See* code of conduct

F

file naming, 78
firewall, 100
front matter, 34, 107

H

home office, 69

I

illustrations, 35, 137
illustrator. *See* artist
indexer, 57, 121
insurance, 104

L

line art, 35, 87
literary agent, 19, 22, 63

M

market study, 30

Index

O

operating system, 66

P

page count, 33, 34, 136
passwords, 103
permissions, 46
photographs, 35, 90
    screen, 90
plagiarism, 27
project editor, 52, 115
promotion, 125
    blogging, 126
    book signing, 127
    reviews, 125
    social media, 126
    speaking, 127
proofreader, 57, 120
proposal, 21, 38
public domain content, 49
purpose of book, 12, 29

R

RACI for publishing, 110
recordkeeping, 45, 50, 74–76, 80–86, 109
research, 45, 75, 132
revisions, 113–22, 134
rights. *See* copyright
royalties, 37, 43–45
    basket accounting, 44

S

schedule. *See* writing schedule
screenshot, 35, 88
second edition vs. second printing, 131
security, 99–104
self-publishing, 40
shelf life, 31, 131
subcontracting. *See* work for hire

T

table of contents, 15, 32–33, 93, 108, 135
tax benefits, 73
tech editor, 26, 53, 95, 116
tech reviewer. *See* tech editor
template, 77
TOC. *See* table of contents
tone. *See* writing voice
Track Changes, 36, 55, 111, 138

U

unboxing, 124

V

vanity publisher, 40

W

word count, 17
working title, 23
writer's block, 97
writing schedule, 36, 73
writing voice, 16

OTHER BOOKS BY PETER H. GREGORY

Gregory, Peter H. CISM Certified Information Security Manager All-in-One Exam Guide. New York: McGraw-Hill, 2018.

Gregory, Peter H. CISA Certified Information Systems Auditor All-in-One Exam Guide, Fourth Edition. New York: McGraw-Hill, 2019.

Miller, Lawrence C.; Gregory, Peter H. CISSP For Dummies, Seventh Edition. Hoboken, New Jersey: John Wiley, 2022.

Gregory, Peter H.; Rogers, Bobby; Dunkerley, Dawn. CRISC Certified in Risk and Information Systems Control All-in-One Exam Guide, Second Edition. New York: McGraw-Hill, 2022.

Gregory, Peter H. Chromebook For Dummies. Hoboken, New Jersey: John Wiley, 2020.

Other Books by Peter H. Gregory

Gregory, Peter H. CIPM Certified Information Privacy Manager All-in-One Exam Guide. New York: McGraw-Hill, 2021.

Gregory, Peter H. CDPSE Certified Data Privacy Solutions Engineer All-in-One Exam Guide. New York: McGraw-Hill, 2021.

Gregory, Peter H.; Hughes, Bill. Getting a Networking Job For Dummies. Hoboken, New Jersey: John Wiley, 2015.

Gregory, Peter H.; Simon, Mike. Biometrics For Dummies. Hoboken, New Jersey: John Wiley, 2008.

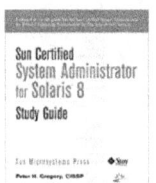
Gregory, Peter H. Sun Certified System Administrator for Solaris 8 Study Guide. Hoboken, New Jersey: Prentice-Hall, 2008.

Gregory, Peter H. Solaris Security. Hoboken, New Jersey: Prentice-Hall, 1999.

The Art of Writing Technical Books

www.ingramcontent.com/pod-product-compliance
Lightning Source LLC
LaVergne TN
LVHW051834080426
835512LV00018B/2863